THE STRENGTHSPATH
Time Manager

DISCOVER YOUR UNIQUE TIME STYLE

DALE COBB

WESTBOW
PRESS®
A DIVISION OF THOMAS NELSON
& ZONDERVAN

Scripture taken from the New King James Version®. Copyright © 1982 by Thomas Nelson. Used by permission. All rights reserved.

This book is a work of non-fiction. Unless otherwise noted, the author and the publisher make no explicit guarantees as to the accuracy of the information contained in this book and in some cases, names of people and places have been altered to protect their privacy.

WestBow Press books may be ordered through booksellers or by contacting:

WestBow Press
A Division of Thomas Nelson & Zondervan
1663 Liberty Drive
Bloomington, IN 47403
www.westbowpress.com
1 (866) 928-1240

Because of the dynamic nature of the Internet, any web addresses or links contained in this book may have changed since publication and may no longer be valid. The views expressed in this work are solely those of the author and do not necessarily reflect the views of the publisher, and the publisher hereby disclaims any responsibility for them.

Any people depicted in stock imagery provided by Thinkstock are models, and such images are being used for illustrative purposes only. Certain stock imagery © Thinkstock.

ISBN: 978-1-5127-6457-4 (sc)
ISBN: 978-1-5127-6456-7 (e)

Print information available on the last page.

WestBow Press rev. date: 2/27/2017

DEDICATION

Thank you to my parents,
Allen and Frances Cobb
who always encouraged me
to pursue my dreams…

And to my beautiful wife and editor
Susy who stood by me when
that wasn't going so well.

CONTENTS

READ THIS FIRST

The purpose of this book is to help you rock time management!

I'm guessing you may have read other books or are aware of other principles, strategies and ideas on the subject. Don't throw any of those suggestions out. This book will allow you to take those other methods and personalize them so that they fit your unique strengths including your passions, talents, personality and values.

I've acquired my knowledge and expertise by studying, experimenting, implementing, reviewing and revising a mass of material from many mentors and role models.

Still, don't let this be the last book you read on time management. These are my insights gathered from hundreds of resources. As you build them around your uniqueness, they should work for you. But let me encourage you to build on the ideas, build better strategies and then let me know so that I can keep getting better as well.

The book is written in a sequence with concepts that are designed to build on each other. But feel free to skip around and cherry pick ideas and start putting the information into action quickly.

PROLOGUE

Time is an unstoppable flowing sequence of events. I tend to think of those events as different size boxes or nesting containers. Probably not as exciting as Einstein's imagining himself riding on a beam of light, but that's how I see it. Time really is a series of gifts. You can decide how to wrap the boxes, although some seem to come pre-wrapped. You can re-wrap them. And you can fill them.

You get to fill those time boxes with activities, energy and effort. You can fill them with purpose, accomplishment, contribution, service, fun, adrenaline, wonderful people and places. You can unpack them and repack them in your imagination before the box actually shows up.

You can pack them tightly. You can pack them with plenty of space. You can leave some of your boxes empty. You can pack them as they come.

This book is written to help you maximize your time or pack your boxes. In that sense it's not unique. A quick visit to your local bookstore or *Amazon* will quickly confirm that. There are hundreds of books available on time management from at least a dozen perspectives. **I believe this is a fresh new perspective**. It is also a perspective that should enhance, not replace all the others.

So you understand what I mean by perspective, let me give you some examples:

The Hebrew Day Planner – If you take the Jewish-Christian Scriptures seriously as I do, the idea of time management is really as old as the first chapter of Genesis itself. As we walk through that first page, we get the idea that God Himself planned His work and worked His plan. He set up efficient systems that reach into every corner of the universe including the intricate workings of the human body. In one sense, automation was first introduced in the book of Genesis. We get the foundation for many time management concepts we work with right here at the beginning of time. And really, time management gems can be gleaned from nearly every book of the Bible, even though it was written over a 1500-year period.

Classic Greek Time Management – Socrates said, "Employ your time in improving yourself by other men's writings so that you shall come easily by what others have labored hard for." I guess that sums up the reason for reading a few time management books. Aristotle and Plato also had ideas with great application to time management today.

Servant Time Management - Broadly speaking this is really "Virtue Oriented" time management. It places service and love as the central virtue at the heart of your time and is largely based on the teachings of Jesus Christ. Modern day management guru Tom Peters affirms this when he writes, "Organizations exist to serve, period!"

Printed Schedule Time Management - This was introduced with the publication of *The Autobiography of Benjamin Franklin* in the late 1700's. Ben identified a routine that worked for him and committed it to paper. John Letts began publishing diaries in the 1800's which proved to be a forerunner to most of what you see at the office supply store today.

Efficiency Oriented Time Management - This was popular during the early 1900's. In the Industrial Economy much emphasis was placed on performing routine tasks in the most efficient manner. Frederick Taylor was arguably one of the first to work in the new profession of management consulting. He took our nation and much of the world down a path of time-motion efficiency studies, concluding there existed a "One Best Way" to do everything. For example, his study concluded that the optimal shovel load was a consistent 21.5 pounds. Companies that drank his *Kool-Aid* modified their issued shovels to accommodate this finding. This made some sense for factory work or any job that involved repetitive tasks.

Efficiency = Task Optimization = Finding and Refining the Right Process.

Technology Oriented Time Management - I guess this one goes back to the discovery of how to make fire and the first wheel. But it really began to multiply in the 1900's. The time management implications of the automobile, the personal computer and the cell phone, to name a few, are staggering. If we were still on typewriters, I wouldn't be writing this. I make too many errors and I need a backspace button. I still remember my early days as a sales rep searching for a phone booth to get my messages.

Effectiveness Oriented Time Management – Peter Drucker began introducing an "Effectiveness" philosophy of time with his writings in the 1950's, 1960's and 1970's. As knowledge work increased, the role of professional manager evolved to a more prominent place in the work picture, and people were routinely required to make choices between tasks. Should I work on this item or that one? While efficient time management meant doing things right, effectiveness meant doing the best task among many choices.

Goal Oriented Time Management - Many of the classic books on time management fall into this category. *How to Get Control of Your Time and Your Life* by Alan Lakein may be the quintessential resource in this group. I love this book. And it should be argued that without goals, time management is pointless.

IV Quadrant Priority Oriented Time Management – First introduced by President Dwight Eisenhower, Stephen Covey did a great job of explaining this one. He divided activities into Quadrants I, II, III and IV including Important, Not Important, Urgent, and Not Urgent. Covey introduced the concept in *The Seven Habits of Highly Effective People*. Then he devoted an entire book to it in *First Things First,* which he co-authored with A. Roger Merrill and Rebecca R. Merrill. Everyone should devour these ideas.

80/20 Time Management - Richard Koch has nailed this one very thoroughly. The work titled *The 80/20 Principle* is just one of his books applying Pareto's famous law to time management. The theory shares how 80% of the results come from 20% of our efforts.

Time Traps - This concept has been covered by Alec Mackenzie, including his research on the top twenty time wasters. The first few include management by crisis, telephone interruptions, inadequate planning, attempting too much, drop-in visitors, etc....

Organizational Time Management - Stephanie Winston's *Getting Organized* has popularized this one. Another book I like is *Order from Chaos* by Liz Davenport. After having said that, David Freedman and Eric Abrahamson have done a great job making a case that order is often not that critical. In their book, *The Perfect Mess*, they provide many examples of successful people thriving in chaos.

Four-Hour Work Week - Tim Ferriss' book has introduced some controversy into the time management mix with other experts weighing in on the viability of his ideas. But Ferriss researches thoroughly and has done everything he advocates. His biggest contributions include ways the small business entrepreneur can utilize automation and technology.

Best Time, Time Management - This moves into some of the more obscure categories. As far as I can see, Mark Di Vincenzo's book, *Buy Ketchup In May And Fly At Noon* introduces this very well. It offers a lot of ideas like "best time to make a presentation", "best day to interview for a job", and "best month to buy a computer". This may sound superfluous but there really are some good tips in this book.

Margin - Richard A. Swenson, M.D. helps with some of our tendencies to take on too much, causing overload resulting in inefficiencies. Swenson offers some great help and ideas. Many time management programs assume we should all be adding more to our plate or getting more done. Sometimes less is more.

Energy Optimization Time Management - Time management is intricately tied to your energy level. Who hasn't experienced an energy drop at 2 in the afternoon? These concepts go into ways to maximize your personal stamina. Jim Loehr and Tony Schwartz offer very helpful advice for those of us who struggle with this area.

Time Shifting - I absolutely loved Stephen Rechtschaffen's book titled *Time Shifting*. He delves into the importance of personal and task rhythms. Each of us have our own internal cadence and beat where we march best. Some of us are punk rockers, some march to the syncopated rhythms of jazz. Tasks and activities also have a unique intrinsic rhythm. And so do our students, staff, co-workers and clients.

The Geography of Time - *Fresno State University* Professor Robert Levine wrote a very well researched book by this title. If you work internationally or even cross-culturally, I recommend this one. Different areas of the world have different values with regard to time. If you work with people from multiple cultures you would be well advised to get your mind around some of the nuances. Susy and I experienced this first hand in Kauai on our honeymoon. Regular business hours just weren't on their radar.

Tool Oriented Time Management - A few of the above categories have time management experts that have developed very useful tools that work with the programs they expound on. *Day Timer* is not listed above but they have provided an awesome integrated suite of tools for decades. *Franklin Planner* and Stephen Covey's organization merged a few years ago to offer a robust group of systems. The proliferation of inexpensive software geared toward time management, including phone apps, is mindboggling.

Getting Things Done (GTD) Time Management - David Allen may currently be the favored time management guru as of this writing. His concepts are a fresh expression and integration of several categories listed above. He has thousands of followers, and some have actually spun off blogs and websites with their own take on his thinking. Allen has authored several books and has a website offering free downloads and programs that elaborate on his ideas. I recommend it all.

Other Resources - Beyond the categories and time management specific gurus, I have scoured and cataloged ideas from biographies and articles from successful people. Lee Iacocca's biography, for example, had some tips. Richard "Mack" Machowicz is a noted author and former *Navy Seal*. His book *Unleash The Warrior Within* has some great tips based on his elite *Special Forces* background.

The *STRENGTHSPATH* Time Management System affirms most of the ideas from all these categories and authors with their unique perspectives. My goal is not to challenge the viewpoints listed above. Rather I hope to offer a new viewpoint, and in fact, offer it as an essential new foundation for the others. If I'm correct, this new foundation will provide an integration point that will harmonize and accelerate the impact of each.

We will take a fresh look at a number of classic time management topics and tips through the lens of your *STRENGTHSPATH*. Strategies and topics like:

Eat the frog first
Procrastination
To-do lists
Blocking time
Goal setting
Planning
Delegation

In some cases there may be good reason to completely overturn conventional time management wisdom. But usually, the *STRENGTHSPATH* approach will slightly modify the classic approaches. Any good <u>individual</u> strategy will begin with the question, "What helps me become the best version of myself?" Any great <u>team</u> strategy begins with the question, "What helps the team become the best version of itself?" Both are strengths oriented questions and where we must begin our approach to time management.

The foundation of this book is intentionally brief and pulled from another book I wrote, *The STRENGTHSPATH Principle*. For a more thorough introduction to strengths, I recommend that book.

INTRODUCTION

STRENGTHSPATH Time Management

The mother of all career development and organizational success questions is, "What Leads To High Performance?" Or some may ask the question, "What gets results?" Or, "How can I be more successful?" If like me, you come from a faith perspective, you may ask, "What produces the most fruit?" And increasingly, more of us are asking for work that is enjoyable, satisfying and fulfilling. Fortunately, enjoyment and effectiveness are mutually reinforcing.

As an entrepreneur, outside sales person, corporate sales trainer, sales manager and career development coach, I've spent most of a lifetime studying the components that lead to high performance. Allocation of time always ranks toward the top. Poor use of time is almost always a key culprit in failure of any kind.

In this short book, I hope to lay out the case that all top achievers have figured out a way to leverage their unique strengths or what I call their *STRENGTHSPATH*. And this *STRENGTHSPATH* dramatically affects effective time use.

Zig Ziglar rightly inspired when he said, "We are designed for accomplishment, engineered for success and endowed with the seeds of greatness."

I completely agree... and I would add that we are:

Designed differently
Engineered uniquely
Endowed with seeds that bloom in varied shades, colors and hues

What Is A *STRENGTHSPATH*?

A *STRENGTHSPATH* is a road, track, route, way or sequence that engages and utilizes your best traits, qualities, attributes, assets and abilities. Your *STRENGTHSPATH* is like an 8 lane super highway that allows you to set a direction, and then reach selected destinations easier and faster with greater enjoyment, efficiency and effectiveness.

Your *STRENGTHSPATH* has a strong neurological basis with a biological foundation. It is based on the idea of super highways or pathways in the brain formed by synaptic connections between neurons or brain cells. Some of these connections are stronger and larger, while others are weaker and smaller. These connections are what create your unique abilities.

Why Strengths Based Time Management?

Your unique mosaic of strengths is foundational to success and satisfaction in virtually every area of your life. This mix impacts the results that you want to get from good time management. Working from your strengths dramatically affects the quality of your time use and nine key productivity components including:

Contribution – Your strengths allow you to maximize the value you add to a company, business unit, client or customer. They explain precisely how you serve best and contribute the most.

Competition – Your strengths are what allow you stand out at work. They set you apart from your competitors. American fashion designer Marc Echo says, "Find your unfair advantage. I'm constantly asking myself, 'What's my unfair advantage?'"

Collaboration – Your strengths are what you bring to the team. Some would argue we are moving into an era where collaboration is more important than competition. Others believe cooperation and competition now go together and have even formed a new word – **Coopetition**, to describe it.

Compensation – Maximize your pay. Your strengths drive your earning potential in any given role. As a rule, the better someone leverages their strengths, the more they contribute over time and the more money they make. Michael Goldhaber said in *Wired* Magazine, "If there is nothing very special about your work, no matter how hard you apply yourself, you won't get noticed, and that increasingly means you won't get paid much either."

Clarity – Defining your strengths will help you set the most authentic goals. Climb the right mountain. Make sure your career ladder is leaning against the right wall. Most people have trouble setting and achieving goals. The biggest reason is that their targets have been disconnected from their talents. Their purpose has been cut off from their passion.

Concentration – Clear authentic goals should lead you to a concentration. We can't be great at everything. A proper understanding of your strengths will allow you to focus on using the unique approaches that will get you to your goals more efficiently.

Contentment - Maximize your satisfaction. Your unique *STRENGTHS ORIENTED PATHWAY* explains the extent to which your work is enjoyable, satisfying and even fun.

Crafting – Jobs never fit perfectly "off the rack". Learn to shape each new assignment so that it better fits your unique abilities.

Course Correction – Defining your strengths will provide a criteria to notice when your career gets off course and a mechanism to get back on track.

Strengths will provide a framework for understanding...

- Failures and successes
- Co-workers
- Teammates
- Supervisors

Exponential Results

The suggestions in this book don't all have equal value. The ideas won't give you the same amount of progress. To borrow from the language of Stephen Covey, there are 3 big rocks in strengths based time management. Once those are placed, the smaller, less important rocks can then be inserted around them:

Strengths – Discovering, Developing and Delivering your passion, talent, personality and values in a way that makes increasingly bigger contributions is the first big rock.

Targets – Working on the signature Dreams, Vision and Goals that flow from your strengths is the second big rock. Strengths-Target disconnect is the single greatest cause of low achievement.

Routes – Using your strengths based signature path is the third big rock. There is a strategy that is designed just for you. It will leverage your signature strengths and will accelerate your progress dramatically.

These 3 rocks will bring you exponential results and accelerate your achievement beyond anything else you can personally do. They will cause you to grow and succeed dramatically! Exponential means by a factor of 10, that is 10x better, bigger, faster. That's what the first three chapters of this book will focus on.

But there is another way of getting better. In addition to the three exponential (Big Rock) strategies, I share time management improvements that are more subtle. Incremental improvement is what the Japanese call Kaizen. The *Toyota Motor Company* reports that they implement one million small improvements in productivity each year. This adds up to huge gains. The rest of this book will be devoted to some smaller ideas and methods that will help you manage your time better. When added together, the results can be substantial. They are based on many of the classic, proven ideas introduced by time use experts over the last century. Most of those techniques can be modified. A strengths based tweak can be added and then we're back in exponential territory.

Exponential gains can also be made each time you make a strengths based hiring decision. Selecting an employee who is passionate about their work and naturally talented for the tasks has a huge payoff. Exponential gains can be made each time you re-position someone who is working outside of their strengths and placing them in their strengths zone. Exponential gains can be made when you help someone re-craft their job so that it is in alignment with their strengths.

Don't get hooked on small improvements. Remember the words of Jesus in the Gospel of Matthew. "You strain at a gnat and swallow a camel." It means, you got all excited about the little things and missed the main thing. This is easy to do in time management. It's easy to do with any area of your life. You can run all over looking for the best calendar and keep the best to-do list, but if you're not working from your signature strengths, moving toward signature destinations and taking signature routes, you won't be maximizing your time.

The central premise of this book is that people naturally manage their time well when they are working from their strengths. Most of the time management programs are designed to help followers muster the discipline to work from weakness. This program begins with your natural strengths and then integrates that philosophy through each piece of your life.

CHAPTER 1

Your Signature Strengths

I define a strength as any resource, internal or external, that helps you make a contribution in the marketplace.

Container Store founder, Kip Tindell says:
"1 Great Employee = 3 Good Employees"

Where and how can you become that great employee? If you're a hiring manager or business owner, how can you hire that next great employee?

If you are working, someone is paying you to add value or make a contribution. That contribution may include:

Speed, Efficiency, Money, Comfort, Beauty, Control, Experience, Safety, Quality, Size, Growth, Knowledge, Skill, Freedom, Delivery, Service, Time, Order, Simplicity, Convenience, Confidence, Leisure, Teamwork or Productivity

The contribution may also include the reduction of:

Risk, Problems, Disease, Illness, Limitation, Difficulty, Debt, Boredom, Chaos, Divisiveness, Poverty, Suffering, Hunger, Depression, Racism, Ignorance or Illiteracy

Adding value is the purpose of your strengths and I will focus on 8 dimensions in this book. Like "facets" on a diamond, or lanes on a super highway, each will cause you to shine in the workplace or succeed in the marketplace. There are several dozen possible categories and components that comprise your unique set of strengths. I cover these strengths with greater detail in my book, *The STRENGTHSPATH Principle.* The 8 Strengths are:

- **Passion**
- **Talent**
- **Personality**
- **Values**
- **Learning Style**
- **Skills**
- **Knowledge**
- **Character**

Let's look at each one briefly:

Passion
"If you're not doing what you love, you're wasting your time."
~Billy Joel

Passion or enthusiasm is a huge time multiplier. It creates energy and attracts others like a magnet. Like world class musician Billy Joel, you might consider much of the work in an activity you're not passionate about, a poor use of time. This component might also be referred to as a natural affinity, appetite, strong interest or desire. Your passion is a topic or task you are drawn to. It's an activity or subject area that makes you feel strong.

I heard Oprah Winfrey share this insight, "Every single person who is super successful always says in some form that following your bliss or **following your passion is the way for you to be the most successful** and empowered person." After forty years of studying human potential, I have to agree.

This does not mean that success is not hard. Steve Jobs told us that it is exactly because success is so very hard that we need to discover our passion. Historically, passion incorporated the idea of suffering. What is it that you love to do so much that you are willing to suffer for it?

I don't believe you will ever manage your time well until you are spending most of your work hours on something that excites you. You can only operate from pure discipline for so long, and then it's exhausting. When you love what you do, you will jump out of bed every morning and will be excited to get to work. And as a result, you will manage your time better. Passion will automatically drive you to work smarter, harder and longer. You will endure failures with comeback after comeback. And that's great time management.

For some, passion discovery is elusive. Sometimes this is fear, disguised as practicality. Following your passion can be a radical act that must overcome pressure from public opinion, parents, partners, professors and promoters. But the discovery process is worth it.

Talent

"I bought my first stock at the age of 11, everything I did before that was a complete waste of time."
~Warren Buffett

A critical dimension of a *STRENGTHSPATH Time Management System* is talent. Simply, it's doing what you naturally do best, the way you best do it! Inter-changeable words are inborn ability, potential or gifts. Talent is what you are naturally good at. Spending time in activities that don't reflect your natural talent is almost always a huge waste of productivity.

There is a myth of "omnicompetence" in both the classroom and the boardroom. You don't have the same potential for success in all arenas. You have a "Talent Triangle" that includes **Aptitudes, Activities** and **Approaches** that drive what you'll be the best at. Trying to work outside of that triangle is one of the biggest wastes of time for most workers.

The first side of our Talent Triangle is **Aptitudes** including:

Words – like communicating, writing and speaking
Numbers – like arithmetic and mathematics
Pictures – like visualizing structures and mechanical objects
Music – like singing or playing an instrument
Body – like coordination and stamina
People – like connecting, befriending and influencing
Self – like awareness and motivation
Nature – like growing plants and raising animals
Existential Thinking - like understanding human purpose

We do not have these aptitudes in the same amounts or combinations. These amounts and combinations are part of what make us unique and allow us to add more value in one arena than in another.

Johnson O'Connor began testing for aptitudes in a *General Electric* laboratory in 1922. He soon after formed the *Johnson O'Connor Foundation* that continues to help individuals make better career choices. They are in most of the major U.S. cities and continue to test for aptitudes like: **Graphoria** – Managing symbols, **Ideaphoria** – Creating ideas, **Structural Visualization** – Thinking in 3 dimensions, **Abstract Visualization** – Manipulating ideas, **Inductive Reasoning** – Seeing connections in scattered facts, **Analytical Reasoning** – Separating into component parts, **Finger Dexterity** – Moving fingers skillfully, **Tweezer Dexterity** - Handling small tools easily, **Observation** – Taking careful notice, **Design Memory** – Memorizing designs rapidly, **Tonal Memory** – Remembering sounds, **Pitch Discrimination** – Differentiating musical tones, **Rhythmic Ability** – Keeping time, **Timbre Discrimination** – Detecting similar pitch & volume, **Number Memory** – Remembering numbers, **Proportional Appraisal** – Discerning harmonious designs, **Silograms** – Learning languages and technical jargon, **Foresight** – Looking into the future with wisdom, **Color Perception** – Distinguishing colors

The second side of our Talent Triangle is **Activities**. On top of our Aptitudes, we all have Activities that are enjoyable and come very easily to us. We have activities where we are AWESOME, activities where we are AVERAGE and activities where we are AWFUL. Spending time on activities that don't allow us to express our underlying aptitudes are usually a waste of opportunity to contribute and add value. In most cases, contrary to popular opinion, trying to get from awful to awesome is a complete waste of time. The effort to get from average to awesome is a poor use of time. Each of us has 3 or 4 activities where we are naturally awesome. Most of our time should be invested in becoming world class at adding value while engaging in those activities.

While there are millions of potential activities and combinations of activities that are potential strengths, our **Activity Talents** will often fall into **Four Types.**

The four include:

- **Activities with People**
- **Activities with Things**
- **Activities with Ideas**
- **Activities with Data/Information**

Think about the four categories above. Is there a little more excitement over one or two categories than the others? Which of the four is your dominant Activity Type? Which is your secondary Activity Type?

Now consider your activities at work. You can focus on current activities, but feel free to draw from past ones as well. Get a sheet of paper or open a word processing document and list everything you currently do in the course of a day/week/month/quarter. Use two lines to create three sections or create 3 text boxes. In the first section, write down activities where your performance is somewhere near **Awesome**. In the second section, **Average**. In the third section, write down the activities where your performance is **Awful**. Consider your performance but also include your passion or enjoyment level. Look for patterns of strength and how well your job really fits. About 25-30% of all workers can optimize a current role by expanding the position in ways that better engage their strengths. Another 25-30% would be more effective if they trimmed a few activities from their work. About 25-30% of workers are altogether miscast for their current role. If this is you... start doing some serious strengths discovery and engage in a full throttle job search.

The third side of our Talent Triangle is **Approaches**. We all have ways of Approaching any activity that works better for us. This is true for any and every role, position or job. In my book, *The STRENGTHSPATH Principle* I talked about the different approaches of stand up comedians, super heroes, U.S. Presidents and later in this book, Supreme Court Justices. In my work as a sales manager and trainer, I noticed very quickly that the best sales reps approached the same job very differently based on their unique mosaic of strengths.

Most of the talent assessments focus on helping individuals better understand their unique approach to a position. Marcus Buckingham's *StandOut* Assessment helps workers activate their unique approach to tasks based on 9 roles. These approaches include: **Advisor, Connector, Creator, Equalizer, Influencer, Pioneer, Provider, Stimulator and Teacher.** The assessment focuses on your top 2 or 3 approaches, while helping you understand in sequence, your lesser strengths.

Gallup's Strengthsfinder 2.0 Assessment helps you understand four approach domains or what I call strength types. These include: **Executing, Influencing, Relationship Building and Strategic Thinking.** *Strengthsfinder 2.0* then gets more detailed or more granular. Each of the four domains has underlying strength themes.

Executing Themes include: Achiever, Arranger, Belief, Consistency, Deliberative, Discipline, Focus, Responsibility and Restorative

Influencing Themes include: Activation, Command, Communication, Competition, Maximizer, Self-Assurance, Significance and Woo

Relationship Building Themes include: Adaptability, Developer, Connectedness, Empathy, Harmony, Includer, Individualization, Positivity and Relator

Strategic Thinking Themes include: Analytical, Context, Futuristic, Ideation, Input, Intellection, Learner and Strategic

Both of these assessments are good first steps to better understanding your most natural approach to any current and future job or position.

Personality

"Your personality style is a kind of map of both your inner geography and the outward direction of your life. You follow its path everyday of your life."
~John Oldham M.D. and Lois Morris

Your personality or temperament is a crucial dimension of *STRENGTHSPATH Time Management.* To effectively manage your time, you must do your work in ways that are harmonious with who you are. Are you a racehorse or plow horse? Both are effective horses, but neither would thrive in the other's role.

People generally behave in patterned, organized and recognizable ways. If we say that someone is outgoing, we usually mean that they are outgoing with some degree of regularity. A pattern is implied. With consistency, we can also say that some traits come packaged together in a unique, yet discernible group that we might call a personality type. Are you more:

Intense or Relaxed?
Shy or Outgoing?
Options Open or Decisive?
Analytical or Active?
Independent or Dependent?
Extroverted or Introverted?
Driven or Carefree?
Cheerful or Serious?
Cautious or Adventurous?
Excitable or Calm?
Leader or Follower?
Friendly or Reserved?
Flexible or Structured?
Detailed or Big Picture?
Sequential or Random?
Quantitative or Qualitative?
Task Oriented or People Oriented?
Fast or Slow?

Each of these traits impact which jobs you will thrive in and which jobs you will dive in. They each impact how **_you_** will work in any role most effectively.

Values
"Make sure your values and the values of the organization are compatible."
~Peter F. Drucker

Your values include your ideals, what's important to you, what you care about, what drives you and what motivates you. If you value a method, a person or object, that means you appreciate and respect them. **Values, when they are aligned, form a group's culture**. Your personal DNA should match the organizational DNA.

If you have a rule, a standard or an ideal, behind it you will find a value. When you use the word "should" there is almost always a value behind it. Families have values. Churches have values. Community service groups have values. Corporations have values. And individuals have values.

All companies have values with regard to things like product quality, speed, beauty, service, customer experience and price point. And in reality they have these values in a sequence, hierarchy or order. No company or customer values them all equally.

In general, your values are a type of strength that should align with the organization and team you are working with. Value conflicts are a huge waste of time.

Here are a list of values I often use as a starting point in my Strengths Clarification work using the acrostic M.Y. B.I.G. D.R.I.V.E.R.S.

Mastery - Growth, Development, Progress, Maturity
Yield - Money, Economics, Rewards, Return, Compensation
Beauty – Aesthetics, Form, Visual Expression
Influence – Authority, Control, Power
Giving – Service, Altruism, Helping
Discovery – Theory, Knowledge, Understanding, Truth
Regulatory – Structure, Order, Routine, Sameness
Individualistic - Independent, Uniqueness, Autonomy

Variety – Change, Newness, Innovation, Creativity
Excellence – Quality, Craftsmanship, Superiority
Relationships – Co-Workers, Collaboration, Team Work
Safety – Security, Protection, Guarantees

Ponder these 12 value themes and threads. Attempt to put them in order according to your own hierarchy. Resist ordering them based on how you think they should be ordered. Then try to do the same with the company where you work. Many top companies are focusing much more heavily on hiring people with matching values. This is smart from a time management perspective. It's really difficult and time consuming to change a person's values. And the same is true for you. Your chances of shifting a company's value set or culture will probably be an exercise in futility, a complete waste of time. Trust me on this. I've tried.

Learning Style

"Lecture continues to be the most prevalent teaching method in secondary and higher education, despite evidence that it produces the lowest degree of retention for most learners."
~David A. Sousa

The next strengths dimension is your learning style. This is your optimal way of perceiving, organizing, retaining and responding to instruction methods. It's a style or pattern of acquiring and processing information.

The ability to learn quickly is at a premium today. The world of work is changing rapidly. Most experts believe the rate of change is accelerating exponentially. This means that entire professions will be replaced after only a few years of existence.

To succeed in the coming world you will need to reinvent yourself many times. That means getting crystal clear on your strongest aptitudes, activities and approaches. It means being ever aware of strengths that may have been laying dormant. And it means being aware of your unique learning style.

How do you learn best? Here is a list of seven different approaches to learning. Each category includes a famous person or type of worker that has displayed a strong preference for the style:

Listening? Franklin Roosevelt, Harry Truman, Lyndon Johnson
Reading? Dwight Eisenhower, John Kennedy, Ben Carson
Doing? Builders, Mechanics, Athletes
Writing? Winston Churchill
Talking? Trial Lawyers, Medical Diagnosticians
Drawing or Sketching? Beethoven
Thinking? *Spanx* Founder Sara Blakely

For each of these styles of learning there are **learning gears**. Learn to use the gear shift within each style. Gear one is deep learning. It means slow, breaking down each piece of information while using one or more of the learning modalities. Gear two happens at a moderate pace. Gear three and above involves summarizing, skimming and scanning. Learn to use all the gears, shifting up and down as the need occurs.

Your learning style is the last of the innate or natural strengths covered in this book. It is the bridge to skills and knowledge which are strengths that must be developed.

Skills

"Since the traits and abilities that we measure do not change with training or coaching, would it make sense to know those before we evaluated skills or purchased training to enhance them?"
~Chuck Russell

Time Management is a skill itself and it must be developed as you progress in your work. But skill development of all types has the potential to improve your time management. Improving your listening skills, clarification skills and presentation skills are all worthwhile investments of time for salespeople, managers or teachers. In fact, to engage any work with underdeveloped skill sets is a horrible misuse of time. Are you performing poorly because you are a poor listener? That's terrible time management. Are you performing poorly because you haven't learned to ask good questions? That's terrible time management. Are you failing because you can't communicate or make clear presentations? That's terrible time management.

Whatever you do for a living, there are corresponding realities. Are you a manager, meat cutter, medical biller or masonry contractor? It doesn't matter what you do, increasing your professional skill level is smart time management! When you build the right skills, you will get a bigger result for the same time and effort.

Spending lots of energy developing the wrong skills is a very common time waster. Make sure that most of your skill development is matched with your underlying talents. A skill will grow much faster and make bigger contributions when it's based on a natural ability.

Some people spend energy building skills that were really better suited for another season of life. When I see 40 year-olds still spending **20 hours a week** trying to improve their baseball skills, while they struggle at their career, I cringe. This is very appropriate for a 16 year-old, but at 40, not so much.

Knowledge

"Knowledge and perception are the result of protracted study and reflection."
~Alban Berg

The right knowledge saves you time. Sometimes that means memorizing, sometimes it means muscle memory, sometimes it means knowing where to look and sometimes it means hiring the person who knows where to look. If you always have to look up the same thing everyday, maybe you should invest the time to memorize it. Or maybe you just need to make the knowledge more accessible. Put the information on a 3x5 card or in a binder nearby.

Knowledge often builds synergy with skill as it works on top of the talent/passion foundation. Where skill is about methods, steps and sequences; knowledge is about awareness and assimilation of principles, rules, information, concepts and facts. In a strengths context, knowledge can be described as an organized body of information, often of a factual nature and sometimes of a procedural nature. It would be a kind of information that would make performing a certain type of work possible. Work is a combination of knowledge and skill. Some roles are more knowledge oriented.

To excel or become world class, you will need to develop expertise. Work on becoming extremely knowledgeable in the area you want to work. Every profession has a unique language that includes vocabulary, terminology, names for parts, pieces and names for equipment or tools. If you are a doctor you will need to learn where each body part is located. If you are a lawyer, learning how the law library is organized and where to look for case decisions and legal precedents is critical. If you are a technology specialist you need to learn where the computer components are located and how they fit together. Salespeople benefit from strong product knowledge. One of my favorite examples is the copier salesperson whose basement was full of copiers, including those of the competition. He knew them all inside and out. He could even make minor repairs to the other company machines as a way of adding extra value up front.

Every profession involves pattern recognition, principles, symptoms, and meaning, along with cause and effect relationships. Knowledge allows you to create "distinctions". When I look inside a computer I say, "Yep, it's a computer!" Hopefully, when my repair person at the *Genius Bar* looks, he or she knows with great precision exactly what each piece is and what it does. Distinction leads to accurate diagnostics. These aren't developable skills so much as they are about building an essential knowledge base.

Whatever work you choose, you will need to develop an awareness and a level of understanding of systems, procedures, equipment, theories, rules, laws, codes, precedents and more. In a world of accelerated knowledge and rapid change, life-long learning becomes a high priority. Learning how to learn is paramount!

Character

"What I call everyday greatness comes from character and contribution."
~Stephen Covey

Character failures undermine success. These failures will undermine the trust you have with clients, partners, peers and supervisors. Consider the following examples:

Most of the U.S. House of Representatives continued to allow themselves insider information privileges on the stock market. A CEO and leaders of a large energy enterprise misrepresented financials, eventually bringing down the entire company and putting thousands out of work. There was the pastor, the parish priest and the football coach. And then there were the brilliant *Wall Street* bankers whose decisions nearly brought down the United States economy, causing millions to lose jobs.

When I write about character strengths, I mean moral qualities and decisions. In fact, character strengths are the ones we all can choose. Consider the following:

Commitment – Attendance, Punctuality, Reliability
Hard Work – Productivity, Diligence, Action, Initiative
Attitudes – Gratitude, Humility, Humor, Cheer, Fun, Mercy
Respect – Authority, Honor, Politeness, Kindness, Fairness
Attention – Present, Alert, Aware, Anticipatory
Courage – Boldness, Bravery, Grit
Truth – Sincerity, Scruples, Trustworthiness, Ethics
Excellence – Workmanship, Quality, Presentation, Hygiene
Restraint – Self Control, Discipline, Clean-Sober, Frugal

Why is character so important? Great successes always require collaboration. Collaboration requires trust. And trust only flourishes where character qualities are pervasive. Stephen Covey has said on a number of occasions, that the American literature on "how-to-be-successful" was mostly about character and moral qualities until the early 1900's. At that point, strategy, technique and tactics began to take center stage. Covey also talks about the **Speed of Trust** in his book by that title. Lack of character leads to mistrust. This slows everything down, including entire world economies. Do you want to move faster? Slow down and take the time to build trust in all your relationships!

CHAPTER 2

Your Signature Targets

"Where are you on the path towards what you really want?"
~Oprah Winfrey

This section is about setting up authentic goals, targets, outcomes or destinations. (I use these terms and others interchangeably throughout the chapter for reasons I will explain later.) To be effective, you must connect your targets to your time use. If you are not trying to get somewhere specific, why would you bother to manage your time in the first place?

Your targets or goals must also flow from your strengths. You must pick, plan and pursue goals that are connected to your natural passion, potential and personality. Most people who are not as successful as they'd like to be, have established targets that are disconnected from their strengths. They are aiming at goals that are not authentic. The strength and target disconnect is the biggest reason most people fail to reach their destinations.

We are all naturally very target oriented. My three month old granddaughter just left our Beach Place loft. She is already setting goals and reaching them. She has goals to get fed. She has goals to get changed. She has goals to be held. As much as she loves her grandma and grandpa, she has goals to get back in her mommy and daddy's arms. Although she has a ways to go, she is vocally communicating and working on forming words. She is working on standing up and will soon be working on various means of cross-the-room transportation.

Goal achievement is the most natural thing in the world. We are **teleological beings** who are directed toward an end and shaped for purpose. In a *USA Today* interview, subjects were polled, "What would you ask God if you got a direct meeting?" By far, the majority of responses were to ask about purpose. "Why am I here?" Or, "What am I here to do?"

Do you struggle with setting goals?
Do you hate setting goals?
Do you fail to reach many or most of the goals you set?

For most of us, the reason is that our goals are not strengths-based...

Our Gifts have been severed from our Goals
Our Aims are not Authentic
Our Targets have been disconnected from our Talents
Our Purpose has been detached from our Passion
Our Vision has no connection to our Values

We must forever give up the idea that most of our goals should be very hard and oriented around forcing ourselves to do things that we don't want to do. I've watched people struggle with setting goals for years. I've struggled with it myself. Targets, to be the most effective, must be formed around your strengths. **In the middle of every bulls-eye, should be a heart to represent your passion and a star to represent your natural talents.**

Some people claim they have no goals... but even living in the moment without a goal is a kind of goal. It's similar to the "psychotics dilemma". Some people go into a fetal position to indicate they don't want to communicate. But what are they doing? They are communicating. It's the same with goal setting. To have no goals, is a goal.

Games

Almost without exception, the activities we seek out as fun, are intrinsically target oriented activities. **Sports are all goal oriented**. Certainly darts and archery are very goal oriented but so is:

Baseball (Strike Zones, Scoring Runs)
Football (Cross the Goal Line)
Basketball (Scoring Baskets, Goal-Tending)
Hockey (Scoring Goals)
Track (Crossing a Finish Line, Running for Time)
Golf (Getting the Ball in the Hole)
Bowling (Hitting the Pins in the Pocket)
Pool (Running the Table)
Swimming (Improving your Time)
Soccer (Scoring Goals)

Board Games are all goal oriented and are a rapidly growing toy category.

Monopoly (Buying Property, Building Houses and Hotels)
Scrabble (Playing High Scoring Words)
Poker (Winning Chips)

Video Games are all goal oriented.

Minecraft
League of Legends
Pokemon

But at Work….

Some of us lose motivation….
Some of us fake motivation…

What happened?

Our Goals Got Disconnected From Our Strengths.

We Are Asked To Play Games We Don't Think We Can Win
or Compete In.

Success

Earl Nightingale told us, "Success is the progressive
realization of a worthwhile goal." Success, however we define it,
is inextricably linked to reaching goals. No goals = no success.
Otherwise, life would be an exercise in shooting an arrow and
running up to draw a target around wherever it lands.

In a world that's rapidly changing, we do need to be
more flexible and open to shifting our goals. Gerald Sindell
writes in his book *Discover Your Genius,* "Our definition of
success needs to be revisited from time to time. While we

are working, creating and innovating, the world also moves on. The goals we set at the beginning of a project begin to age from the moment we set them. Every few weeks or months, we need to determine whether what we have been working toward is tied to a time and context that no longer exists. Fuel costs can change everything. Tastes change. Other innovations create constantly evolving environments. The intended audience we began with may not be the same audience that we will be trying to reach when we're ready to go to market. Finally, not only will our intended user change, but also our project itself will change as we develop it. As we move along on our project, we will need to determine whether our definition of success needs to expand our contract. Perhaps our original goals were overly ambitious and we can now see that we cannot possibly reach all of our initial goals with this particular project. It is also possible that our breakthroughs have been so audacious that we can expand our horizons, do more for our user than we had originally hoped, or reach a larger audience."

Sindell continues, "If we define success inaccurately, we face the danger of achieving the wrong success. Imagine we are building a race car. If we define our goal as going faster, then everything we do will be aligned with whatever it takes to inch up our speed. But if we define our goal as winning races, then we will embrace everything involved, from suspension, to driver vision to endurance."

Target Style

"Talent hits a target no one else can hit. Genius hits a target no one else can see."
~Arthur Schopenhauer

Not only should our goals be built around our strengths, especially our passion and talents, but we each need to find a style of goal setting that works for us.

Traditional target people are more into the classical model of setting up outcomes. They have lifetime goals, 10-Year Goals, 5-Year Goals, 1-Year Goals, Quarterly-Goals, Monthly-Goals, Weekly-Goals and Daily-Goals. I encourage everyone to try this model and see how it works for them. It may work very well in one area of your life and not so well with others. Many organizations have been structured around this goal setting model and it has advantages.

Traditional Targeting

"People are not lazy. They simply have impotent goals – that is, goals that do not inspire them."
~Tony Robbins

Many employees hate top down management by objectives where the leadership sets all or most of the goals for employees. Often workers keep quiet about this dislike unless trust has been built with their direct supervisor. I managed an individual for many years. He was by far the top producer on my team and one of the top earners in the entire company, consistently pulling in over 100K each year. He also had a "hobby business" on Saturdays. Believe it or not, he earned even more per year at his hobby. He won nearly every award the company had to offer and did it year in and year out. Although he was pegged as laid back in the home office, he was probably earning more than the corporate Vice-Presidents in total yearly income. He was a huge achiever, but he absolutely hated company goal setting.

Why is that? Why would someone so dedicated, so committed and so successful, hate goal setting so much? He also turned down promotion after promotion. I think this was partially because his earnings would have been cut by about 75%, especially if forced to give up his "hobby business". But I think part of it was because he knew that a management position would drag him into the world of continual goal setting.

What's the problem? The problem is that many companies regularly use targets to hype employees up, and then beat them up. Management always wants more. I've heard it hundreds of times. The purpose of a company is to grow. I loved growth, both as a sales rep, a sales trainer and a manager. Healthy things including businesses grow. But healthy growth is a nurturing organic individualized process that doesn't respond well to hype and threats.

Targeting can be an exciting part of the growth process. People are natural born goal setters. But it's too often beaten out of them. Used poorly, it turns fun work into something people dread.

I'm not asking you to stop setting goals or achieving goals. I spent a year working in the *Zig Ziglar* organization. He sold me on goal setting. Companies need to forecast for legitimate reasons. They need to plan purchases and hire. But if you are in a supervisory position, I am asking you to be more flexible in how you talk about goals and set up different styles of targeting, incorporating the unique preferences of each employee. And be more aware of your own signature style of goal setting. One size doesn't fit all when it comes to setting up strong targets.

River People

There are other goal setting models. Earl Nightingale also talks about river people. Nightingale writes, "These are men and women who have found, often early in life, although not always, a great river of interest into which they throw themselves with exuberance and abandon. They are quite happy to spend their lives working and playing in that river. For some, the river may be a particular branch of science; for others, one of the arts. There are some physicians, for example, who are so wrapped up in medicine that they hate to leave; even after a 16 hour day, they can't wait to get back to it. These people are happiest and most alive when they're in their river in whatever business or career or profession it happens to be. And success comes to such people as inevitable as a sunrise. In fact, they are successes the moment they find their great field of interest; the worldly trappings of success will always come in time. Such people don't have to ask, 'What will I do with my life?' **Their work is a magnet for them, and they can't imagine doing anything else.** We all know such people, or about such people. Doing what they do is even more important to them than the rewards they earn for doing it."

For some successful people, they focus almost exclusively on the task in front of them. Diane Sawyer, Frances Hesselbein, Ellen Barkin and Lori Greiner tend to fall in this category. They are more project oriented and don't have the lifetime goals broken down in segments and categories. They may even claim not to have goals at all, but clearly they do.

In a 1997 interview with *US Magazine*, journalist Diane Sawyer said, "I've never had a career plan and never will. I just always make sure that I'm doing something I love at the moment, and I find out where it takes me. I float down river, then I wake up and say, 'Oh, here I am. I've had a swell float.'" That sure sounds like Nightingale's "River Person"!!!

In a June 8, 2016 interview with *Parade Magazine*, actress Ellen Barkin said, "I was just working, putting one foot in front of the other diligently. I'm not a big goals person. I didn't have big goals as a young woman, or a middle-aged woman or an older woman. I'm doing it until I don't want to do it anymore." Clearly, Ellen Barkin does have goals. She takes on movie projects and she completes them very professionally. She researches the role and learns the lines for each script. These are very specific goals. Ellen's goals just don't go much past the current project.

Painter Pablo Picasso once told a friend, "I don't know in advance what I am going to put on the canvas anymore than I decide beforehand what colors I am going to use. Each time I undertake to paint a picture, I have a sensation of leaping into space. I never know whether I shall land on my feet."

Author Isabel Allende says about writing her books, "In a very organic way, books don't happen in my mind, they happen somewhere in my belly. I don't know what I am going to write about because it has not yet made the trip from belly to mind."

This idea of spontaneous goal-setting is driving some of you crazy. It's a form of heresy! I can hear you grinding your teeth. But this is a legitimate way of targeting for some people. It is how they are wired and work most effectively.

How about a "Scouting Story"? Scouting is all about setting goals, right? Maybe not for *Girl Scout*, CEO Frances Hesselbein who claims, "I never had the ambition to do any of the things I've accomplished. In fact, for most of my jobs, I didn't knock on a door. I was thrown through the door! But once inside, I realized that was where I was supposed to be." Hesselbein was perhaps one of the most transformational leaders of our time. Once she was, "thrown through the door", she clearly set organizational goals. But she really had no intention of landing any of the lofty positions she attained. ...More teeth grinding from you classically trained sales managers...I hear you!

Entrepreneurs have clearly defined goals... Lori Greiner is a coach on TV's *Shark Tank* and the Queen of *QVC*. Lori describes her path to entrepreneurship, "I never really set out to be an entrepreneur, nor did I ever take a business class. I just was always thinking of ideas."

Path People

"There go my people. I must run and catch up with them, because I am their leader!"
~Mahatma Gandhi

Architects and landscapers have a strategy they use when laying walkways. After the building is designed and erected with the traditional blueprint to build sequence, they lay out the basic landscape but leave off the walking paths. They plant grass and then pay careful attention to where it gets worn down by feet traipsing across the grounds. This highlights the natural pathways. Only then do they plan and add the concrete or pavers. The architects allow people to decide where they want to walk and then they build the concrete walkways to match.

This path of least resistance strategy clearly has a place in your goal setting arsenal. It's experimental, open, consensus building and even democratic. It's a way of gathering real life input on what is wanted, needed and what will really work. It's a form of listening.

Many who are natural goal setters and achievers in the more traditional model fail to get enough input. In traditional project models, upper management tells the team how long the project will take. This lack of feedback from team members actually doing the work, always leads to cost and time overruns. In many cases, top down management by objectives is inaccurate and inefficient.

In the *Agile* model, which I will cover later in the book, there is an approach to project time estimating where the team all submits guesstimates for each project increment. This inclusive approach is what I recommend for anyone who wants to maximize their success.

Serendipity People

The word "serendipity" was coined by Horace Walpole in 1754. He was fascinated with a Persian fairytale in which three princes of Serendip, (now Sri Lanka) traveled the world, "making discoveries, by accidents and wisdom, of things **not** included in their quest." Walpole proposed the new word, but then went on to give rather mundane examples of its meaning.

Richard Eyre suggests, *"Serendipity* is using alertness and wisdom to discover things that are far better than what you are seeking. **It is the faculty for finding something fantastic while seeking something else**. Serendipity involves a certain combination of awareness, observation, acceptance, and optimism that lets us find the best in whoever we are with, whatever is going on, wherever we are, wherever we are living, and however we are feeling. In all cases we are finding and flowing instead of forcing and fighting."

David Allen is perhaps the most popular time management guru of our day. He writes, "How much do I 'let things happen' as they might, trusting that the world and my life in it are flowing onward in a natural way; and how much should I set my own goals and objectives, and march toward them with conscious determination and effectiveness?... I have discovered there is no answer to that as long as I have the question. And I only have the question when I have been ignoring my own inner quiet place for too long. When I let go of my attention on this world and let myself drop back into the subtler and larger places I have access to, the questions fade away. I find myself in the paradoxical state of surrendering to the larger flow and consciously creating my next directions and outcomes. There are times for me to let things just show up, and respond. There are times for me to make it up and make it happen. I just need to pay attention to the music. And when I do, it's all the same dance."

Columbus was looking for India when he discovered America.

Alexander Graham Bell was trying to invent a device that would help the deaf when he invented the telephone.

Peter, James, John, and the other disciples were looking for a Messiah that would overthrow the harsh Roman Government and found a Messiah that established a much more powerful Kingdom of the Heart.

Sir Alexander Fleming discovered penicillin when he left a window open and the wind blew contaminants on his staphylococcus culture.

The X-ray was born when Wilhelm Roentgen was experimenting with electricity and vacuum tubes.

These are true examples of serendipity!

Solution People

"The greatest gift God will ever give you is a problem you were made to solve."
~David Foster

Some very successful people just don't relate to the goal setting language or frame. Bobb Biehl is a very successful management consultant who worked with organizations all over the country. I was first introduced to Bobb's ideas at one of his *Plan Your Life in a Day* workshops back in the 1980's. Bobb was a dedicated goal setter in the traditional sense and had been teaching it for over 25 years. His "Eureka" revelation came when he was working with *Dave Ray and Associates*, an electronics firm in Troy, Michigan.

Bobb was a strengths-based consultant well before it was popular. He started off the session with the *Dave Ray* executive team with a question, "What is your single greatest strength? What do you do the very best?" He then went around the room asking each individual to share their top strength. Approximately half of the team shared that their strength was "reaching goals". The other half said, "solving problems".

Bobb says, "It was as though, in one fraction of a second of insight, twenty years of frustration (trying to teach goal setting to problem solvers) made complete, 100 percent sense. Bobb started teaching a new program and later wrote a book, *Stop Setting Goals If You'd Rather Solve Problems.* Then he began to get feedback like:

"This has been one of the freest days of my life."

"I have hated setting goals as long as I can remember, but I love solving problems."

"When I am forced to set goals, I find myself wanting to come to work late and leave early."

"I no longer feel like a second-class citizen."

Bobb asks, "How much energy is lost because problem solvers are stuck on goal setting teams? How many multiplied millions or even billions of dollars are wasted daily because demotivated problem solvers are forced to set goals?"

I see this a little differently than Bobb does. From my perspective, problem solving is just a specialized form or sub-set of goal setting. But the point is, so many in our culture have had goal setting forced on them in a way that doesn't fit who they are.

Changing the language may help some people. Tony Robbins, who was trained in *Neuro-Linguistic Programming* (*NLP*), after tons of exposure to classical goal setting under the training of Jim Rohn and others, rarely uses the word goals. He talks about outcomes and results. Stephen Covey, in his book, *Seven Habits of Highly Effective People*, talks about, "Beginning With The End In Mind". It took me a while to realize what they were even talking about. If you struggle with goal setting, it may help to connect with an author or speaker that has changed the language.

Mission People

"Everyone has his own specific vocation or mission in life; everyone must carry out a concrete assignment that demands fulfillment. Therein he cannot be replaced, nor can his life be repeated, thus, everyone's task is unique as his specific opportunity to implement it. We detect rather than invent our mission in life."

~Victor E. Frankl, Holocaust Survivor and Author of *Man's Search For Meaning*

Some will resonate much more strongly with the idea of mission than the concept of a goal. If this is you, embrace it!

Mother Theresa was on a mission of mercy.
Martin Luther King Jr. was on a mission of justice.
Albert Einstein was on a mission to understand the universe.
Jonas Salk was on a mission to eradicate polio.
Abraham Lincoln was on a mission to preserve the union.
Winston Churchill was on a mission to save England.
Nelson Mandela was on a mission to establish equality in South Africa.

Zig Ziglar said, "Outstanding people have one thing in common: an absolute sense of mission."

Zig's right. I also believe Churchill was right when he said, **"To each, there comes in their lifetime, a special moment when they are figuratively tapped on the shoulder and offered the chance to do a very special thing, unique to them and fitted to their talents."**

I believe everyone on the planet has a purpose. We were all made with a mission in mind. And if you're alive, you are not finished fulfilling that mission. I have always had a sense of destiny. It hasn't always been clear and focused, but it's been there never the less. I believe that everyone has a destiny. You may deny it. You may be out of touch with it. You may run from it. But it's there.

Your mission or purpose isn't to be famous. Your mission or purpose isn't to be rich. You may become both in the process of fulfilling your mission but that's not the mission. **Your mission is to serve. It will always be about helping someone else. Your true purpose will always benefit others.** And your mission will grow out of your absolutely unique mix of passion, talent, personality, values, skills, knowledge and character. It will all fit together perfectly.

It may not look like a mission at first. It may look like an insurmountable problem. It may look impossible. My mission is helping others recognize and then realize their unique God-given potential, to get in alignment with their assignment. It's helping people find or create the work they are designed to do. It seems overwhelming. It's a daunting task. Upwards of 80% aren't even close. Upwards of 80% are on the "Thank God It's Friday Track". Upwards of 80% have that Monday-Morning-Sick-Feeling because they're not doing what they're supposed to be doing.

What do you want to accomplish? Let me ask it a different way. What do you have to accomplish? Do you have a mission?

Micro-Missions

Maybe it's raising three kids to make character based choices in a culture that's pulling on the wrong end of the rope every single day.

Maybe it's organizing a group of Moms-on-a-Mission or Marriages-on-a-Mission or Men-on-a-Mission.

Maybe it's teaching toddlers or tutoring teenagers on how to take better care of their body.

Maybe it's joining a team and working in support of someone else's mission.

Maybe it's picking up trash in your neighborhood with a group of "Eco-cisers" on morning walks.

Maybe it's joining the Air National Guard, keeping our fighter jets operational and our country safe.

Maybe it's organizing a group for young adults whose mission is to pray for the Kingdom of God on Earth.

Maybe it's pulling together 50 years of experience and starting a jobs program.

Maybe it's mentoring marriages that are struggling to make it.

Maybe it's teaching a class on financial principles so other people won't make the same mistakes you did.

Maybe it's starting a church for people who have been hurt by church or bored by church.

Maybe it's putting makeup on people who want to look their best on a special day.

Maybe it's capturing snapshots of time on a photograph.

Dreams

Targets begin with dreams. I'm convinced everyone has dreams but many have faced disappointments, discouragement and defeats that have disconnected them from their authentic dreams. Most of us have been encouraged to live dreams that are not our own. Others have been told that their authentic dreams were not possible by people in authority. Still others were encouraged to dream, but to take pathways that didn't fit. Many multi-level marketing companies have been guilty of this last one. These companies are great at encouraging their sales people to dream big dreams. But they recruit everyone, regardless of their interest or talent for selling. Most people who enter multi-level marketing fail quickly. The failure is internally associated with the encouragement to dream big dreams. Many never dream again.

If any of the above scenarios explain your relationship with dreaming, I'm going to encourage you to dream again. But this time, find the pathway, the *STRENGTHSPATH* toward those dreams. In fact, as with the "River People" described earlier, *the river itself may be the dream*.

Miley Cyrus sings, *It's The Climb*. Some are more interested in climbing the right mountain than getting to the top. Jim Hayhurst, Sr. wrote a brilliant book on this topic called, *The Right Mountain – Lessons from Everest On the Real Meaning of Success*. Jim is the founder of *Outward Bound Canada*. He didn't complete his original goal of climbing Mt. Everest, but instead decided to stay back and help others reach the summit. In a sense, that's what anyone who goes into management or coaching does. They decide they are wired to help others succeed.

None of the great coaches in sports history were great individual performers or athletes. They came to realize that their big successes would come by helping others achieve.

I grew up hearing a saying, ""Those who can... do. Those who can't... teach." It was intended to be a swipe at the teaching profession. Actually, teaching and coaching are unique, important and legitimate ways of doing.

Calling All Dreamers

Artisanal – What kind of life do I want to create?
Spiritual – What kind of faith do I want to have?
Biblical – How do I want to align more with the teachings of scripture?
Teleological– How do I want to manifest my design and destiny?
Contributional – How do I want to add value and serve?
Solutional – What problems do I want to solve?
Alchemical – What do I want to transform, create or combine?
Transformational – How do I want to change?
Cultural – How do I want to transform our culture?
Aptitudinal – How do I want to deliver my talents?
Mental – What thoughts do I want to think?
Emotional – How do I want to feel?
Motivational – What values and priorities do I want to honor?
Inspirational – What passions and deep desires do I want to honor?
Attitudinal – What attitudes and beliefs do I want to hold?
Amygdaloidal – How do I want to better manage my emotions?
Analytical – What do I want to think about more?
Volitional – What choices do I want to make?
Behavioral – What habits and patterns do I want to build?
Physiological/Postural – How do I want to position my body?
Physical – What kind of energy/exercise/eating will I incorporate?
Medical – What do I want to get fixed or healed?

Developmental – What skills/character qualities do I want to develop?

Intellectual – What do I want to read, listen to, watch and learn?

Educational – What training and knowledge do I want to acquire?

Informational – How will I stay informed?

Conversational – Who do I want to meet and stay in touch with?

Missional – What contributions and value do I want to offer?

Reputational – What do I want to be known for?

Recreational – What kinds of fun do I want to have?

Experiential – What do I want to experience?

Financial – How much money do I want to save, spend and share?

Material – What do I want to purchase/own?

Occupational – What do I want to do for work?

Professional – What do I want to accomplish in that occupation?

Indispensable – How will I meet critical needs?

Charitable – What organizations do I want to support?

Promotional – How do I want to influence other people?

Relational/Social – What kind of friend do I want to be?

Marital – What kind of marriage partner do I want to be?

Parental – How do I want to treat my parents?

Maternal/Paternal – What kind of mother/father do I want to be?

Model – Who do I want for role models, mentors and advisors?

Tribal/Communal – What groups do I want to join?

Geographical – Where do I want to live, work and serve?

Environmental – What do I want to surround myself with?

Architectural – What kind of home do I want to live in?

Travel – Where do I want to visit?

Global – How do I want to impact the planet?

National – How do I want to influence my country?
Local – How do I want to impact our area?
International – How do I want to impact other countries?
Political – How do I want to influence the system?
Eternal/Global – What kind of legacy do I want to leave?
Miracle – Where do I need God to show up?

Signature Goal Setting

Parker Palmer, founder of *Center for Courage & Renewal* says, "Before I can tell my life what I want to do with it, I have to listen to my life telling me who I am." There is an important sequence in goal setting and then in managing time... **Being – Doing – Having...**

Much of your **Being**, including your unique blend of passion, talent, personality, values and learning style are established either at birth or very early in life. You can continue to maximize each, by adding skills and knowledge that build on those innate traits throughout life. The **Doing** includes tasks and activities that flow out of your Being when you are performing optimally. David Viscott said, "Your ultimate goal in life is to become your best self. Your immediate goal is to get on the path that will lead you there." When you get Being and Doing aligned, the **Having**, (the results and rewards) flow much more easily and naturally.

All of us can be developing our own signature goal setting strategy that is built around our signature strengths. That includes the terminology we use. I love the word **dream**. I like **target** because it causes me to imagine a bright red symbol. Maybe you like the words **outcome**, **objective**, **intention**, **result** or **beginning with the end in mind**. Use a word that resonates with you.

What is your natural style of goal setting? Are you a **river person** who just needs to throw yourself into an interest? Are you a **path person** who prefers listening and consensus building? Do you prefer **solving problems**? Set aside everything you've heard about goal setting for a moment and make up your own approach.

I am very project oriented and don't do as well with longer term targets. Think about your signature distance or time frames. Tim Ferris, the author of *The 4-Hour Work Week* is a committed goal seeker. Yet Tim's approach to goals is clearly out of the mainstream from most of the classical teaching on the subject. Tim shared in an interview with *Success Magazine*, "I don't have 5 or 10 year professional goals. I have 3-6 month experiments. I don't know what door is going to open. I don't chase what makes me happy. I seek out and chase the things that excite me."

If goal setting is a struggle for you, start with a day. Start with the next 60 seconds if you have to. Set goals in very short time frames and gradually work your way out until you find a frame that fits you. Different kinds of targets can lend themselves toward specific time frames. For example, weight loss goals often work best in one-week segments. Single day weight loss goals are impacted by water retention and elimination variables.

On the other end of the spectrum, Dan Sullivan has a whole system for entrepreneurs built around a 25 year time frame. This is far beyond the 5 to 10 year segments suggested by the classical teaching on setting goals. Dan says, "The reason why you're stressed out and that you don't have enough time, is that your deadlines are too short and the time frame is too narrow." He continues, "I don't think there are unreasonable goals in this world, I do think there are unreasonable time frames."

Design a goal achieving system that fits who you are. Our destinations should be based on our own signature design. Both your mission and your methods will ideally grow out of your innate strengths.

CHAPTER 3

Your Signature Routes

*"To be successful you can't just run on the fast track, you must run on **your** track."*
~John Maxwell

Great time management that leads to amazing achievements begins with the discovery and development of your signature strengths. The next step is to discover and develop your signature targets or goals. In this section we want to look at our signature routes. Not just how to best get from point A to point B, but what is the best way for us individually? Our routes, our methods or our strategies need to fit us just as much as the goals we set. Our routes will be the most effective if they are strengths based.

Routes need to be continually re-evaluated. As Tony Robbins says, "You've got to constantly re-evaluate your strategy because a lot of people are all pumped up and excited and they're passionate but they are running east looking for a sunset." We all need to regularly ask, "Am I on a path that will get me to my signature destination?" And we also need to ask, "Am I on the right path for me?" A great track for one person is just a merry-go-round for another. Marcus Buckingham has suggested, "The most efficient route from point A to point B is rarely a straight line; it is always the path of least resistance. Try to find each person's path of least resistance to performance."

We're not always looking for the fastest route. If the mountain climbers scaling Mount Everest were looking for the fastest route, they would take a helicopter. We are looking for the routes that get us to our signature destinations in the most authentic way.

Your Directions, Maps, GPS and Compass

As an outside sales rep, I have driven around in circles a few times. As a sales manager and trainer on ride-a-longs, I've not only been taken in circles, I've gotten dizzy. Contrary to popular opinion and urban legend, it's not just men who won't stop and get directions. There is no bigger waste of time and energy than driving around looking for an address.

There are so many good options to avoid this and there are more coming out all the time. Personally I don't care for maps...especially the old paper kind that I could never get re-folded correctly. Laminated maps are better. *Thomas Guide Books* had a season of superiority although it was difficult to get the big picture and how everything fit together. Eventually I moved to *Microsoft Streets & Trips* and then *MapQuest* and *Google Maps*.

Today, GPS is probably the quickest and most efficient way to get anywhere. A decade ago, the first time I ever rode with a marketing rep who had GPS in his car, I was amazed at the time savings and efficiencies. He was a relatively new rep with no way of knowing his territory that well. Yet he navigated between accounts quicker than many reps who have been in their territories for years. GPS was a huge step forward.

Of course, from a destination and time management perspective, these tools can be symbols for the kind of tools we might use for career and life planning. The compass may still be the optimal symbol to get started with designing our own signature route. Each of us has an internal compass represented by our innate passions, talents, personality, values, learning style and now our signature dreams and destinations. This internal compass will also point us to the most authentic route. Spiritually, we may select a North Star, a fixed point to orient us when we get lost. The North Star I've selected is Jesus Christ.

Maps are helpful tools. I'm spatially challenged, so maps have always been a bit of a struggle, but they help us understand context and the story we find ourselves in. When I previously used a physical map, I found it helpful to plot out my path and then actually write out point-to-point, step-by-step directions. *Google Maps* will do that for you today. Step-by-step routing is still helpful for other kinds of life and career journeys. In selling, I've put together a kind of step-by-step map that I use for sales presentations. I call it, *A-Game Selling* and I'm writing a book about it now. The basics are Add-Approach-Align-Access-Advise-Assure-Agree. These steps provide me with a road map to selling in a way that always adds value to a client or customer.

Route models or road models can be useful in finding our own path. Although we are unique, one-of-a-kind miracles, there are other individuals that are similar to us. They have a similar mosaic or make-up of passion, talent, personality, values and even learning style. With some research and practice, you can seek out people who have similar strengths, but are already succeeding and a few steps further down the road. Learn from their route as you figure out your own.

Planning Your Daily Route

Many people benefit from planning their day in writing, either electronically or on paper. You can change your plan, but get it in writing somehow. I find it better to plan in 7-day weeklong blocks. At one point in history, the ever inventive French tried to change a week to 10 days. It didn't work. When he was with *Chrysler Motor Company*, Lee Iacocca planned his week out every Sunday night. Stephen Covey was a big fan of planning in weeklong segments as well. If Sunday doesn't work for you, do it on Saturday or even Friday afternoon. The night before, you can fine tune the plan further or make changes or adjustments as needed. In some cases you might need to scrap a plan altogether. Much of the decision to focus on planning monthly, weekly or daily should be based on how you are wired, not on someone's cool system.

The benefit of any plan or route is not necessarily the plan itself but the thinking that is required in making a plan. Beyond that, a plan gives you a track to run on until something comes along that requires an adjustment. I find even **successful people vary quite a bit in how much they are willing to adjust a plan.** Some are inflexible and stick with their plan no matter what. Some are more opportunistic and shift when they see a good possibility.

In some communities, working the traffic flow and rush time properly can easily save you 2 to 3 hours of a day. Every bit of this can be re-invested in more productive activity. Where you choose to live in relationship to your territory, can have a tremendous influence on this.

The Nashville Principle

There is a strengths based geography of success that involves signature destinations and time management routing. One I call the "Nashville Principle" or "Taylor Swift Strategy". As a teenager, Taylor Swift decided she wanted to be a music star. She talked her parents into moving the whole family to Nashville. Taylor had decided her path went through Nashville and her parents agreed. Sometimes you can't get to your signature destination from where you are. You'll have to move.

Leadership expert, John Maxwell made a similar decision. He lived in San Diego with a near-paradise climate. But he looked at his strengths oriented signature direction of delivering keynote speeches every week. He looked at where most of the signature target organizations were located and he moved his whole company to Atlanta, Georgia. He freed up hours on his schedule that allowed him to crank out books and have more time with his wife Margaret.

Your Daily Routines

"The secret of your success is determined by your daily agenda."
~John Maxwell

Routes may vary a great deal from month-to-month, week-to-week or day-to-day, but I find that most successful people develop a strengths based routine that fits them like a glove and they tend to stick with it. I've been collecting summaries of these strengths based routines for over a decade and they are fascinating. Benjamin Franklin believed, "Early to bed and early to rise, makes a man healthy, wealthy and wise." One our family members asks, "Why is sleeping in lazy, but going to bed early is not?" With all due respect to Ben Franklin, she's right. My research shows huge swings in how successful people schedule a day.

Winston Churchill started at noon and worked from bed.
Albert Einstein woke up at 8am and was walking before 9am.
Issac Newton rarely went to bed before 2 or 3am.
Michael Jordan shot hoops at 6am during high school.
Kobe Bryant, with the *Lakers*, would be working out by 4am.
Comedian **David Brenner** started reading newspapers at 3pm.
Oprah was up around 5am and at work by 6:30 or 7am.
Howard Schultz is up and walking the dogs at 4:30am.

Dilbert creator Scott Adams says, "Nothing is more important to my success than controlling my schedule. I'm most creative from five to nine a.m. If I had a boss or co-workers, they would ruin my best hours one way or another."

Drive author Daniel Pink believes that few things are more important than autonomy or the ability to schedule one's own work in one's own way.

I'm writing a book with the working title, *Strong Days,* documenting the routines of successful people. In the meantime, I recommend Mason Currey's *Daily Rituals – How Artists Work*. He goes over the daily routines of 161 famous artists. It's an eye-opener!

Establishing a daily routine that fits you may be the biggest thing you can do for your success and improve your time management. Some progressive companies are recognizing this and offering flex-time, unlimited vacation days and other time customization opportunities. *3M* has allowed technical staff to spend 15% on any product they choose. It was during this 15% time that Art Fry came up with the Post-It Note. Today *3M* offers nearly 600 Post-It note products. Employees at *Google* get 20% of their work time or approximately one day a week to use on side projects. Paul Bucheit created *Gmail* during his side project time. You could make a case that most of *Google's* growth has been fueled by people working outside their primary role.

This is not an invitation to just start showing up for work whenever the mood strikes. It's an invitation to do some serious career planning.

Bottom Line - When you're good at something, and enjoy doing it, make it a habit and a big part of your daily routine.

Your Core Activity

In the movie *City Slickers,* there was a famous dialogue between Jack Palance (Curly) and Billy Crystal (Mitch Robbins) as they ride along on horse back:

Curly: Do you know what the secret of life is?
Mitch: No, what?
Curly: This. (Holds up one finger)
Mitch: Your finger?
Curly: One thing, just one thing.
Mitch: That's great but, what's the one thing?
Curly: That's what you've got to figure out.

Every job and every business has that one thing. It's a core payoff activity that is absolutely critical to success. It doesn't mean you don't have other important activities to attend to that move you toward success. It does mean that there is one that is critical to focus on. Successful people figure this out early on in their career and keep it front and center.

If you are in sales, I can pretty much say with confidence that your core payoff activity is being with customers creating business. If you think I am wrong on this, check with your manager.

If I'm right, you should build your whole career and time management system around this activity. Anything less and you will be short changing yourself, your company, and your family.

Great selling is all about great serving. Serve more people. Serve better people, that is, those people who can afford and benefit from your product or service. And then serve people better. Make your presentations more clear, more concise, more compelling.

If you're a writer, spend more time writing. Focus on the right audience. Get better at writing.

Jim Fannin is a coach who works with elite level athletes in multiple sports as well as high level performers from the business world. In his book, *S.C.O.R.E.,* Fannin talks about the importance of understanding, "The Essence of Your Craft". He worked several years with baseball all star Alex Rodriquez and began with this understanding – "You hit the core of the ball on the sweet spot of your bat with an accelerated barrel." I've played a lot of baseball and I don't know how you could improve on that. When working with car salespeople, they begin with the understanding that they – "motivate people to improve the quality of their transportation at a price they can afford".

Every job has a core activity with an essence of the craft. **Does the core activity of your work match your core strength? For most people it doesn't.** Making that shift is what strengths based time management is all about. For some, that will be a subtle shift, tweaking, expanding or contracting a job so that it fits. For others, it means career change.

Your Controlling Insight

What's the Big Idea of your job? The core activity in a job leads to the controlling insight. I worked 18 years in a sales role and then a sales management and trainer role. The controlling insight was being in front of prospective clients who could sign new business between the hours of 9am and 1pm. Everything was designed around being in the first prospect's parking lot by 8:30 am. After 2pm, and into the evening, we were serving existing customers with follow-up training and coaching.

Representatives who did this well were generally very successful. Those who didn't live by this controlling insight either weren't as successful or failed altogether.

Some of this was an issue of self-discipline. It was about building a weekly/daily routine around the core activity. From a strengths perspective, the success was about how well those two activities, in the two time frames, matched up with the rep's natural passion and talent. The better the match, the bigger the success.

In my experience, there is a corollary to this in every type of work. The hours may change, the work shifts may be more flexible, but it's about a repeatable routine and a match of strengths with tasks.

The core activity and controlling insight is the center piece to any role. In our case, there was more to the job. We had about 40 other tasks that had to be completed. Everything from checking voicemail, email, crafting responses, doing expense reports and drive times had to be factored in. Every role has non-central but essential details.

Your Positional Prime Time

Every position or role has a prime time. This is defined as a window that is disproportionately effective in performing a core payoff activity. In my outside selling, the core payoff activity was calling on prospective customers for the purpose of securing new business. In my industry, prime time was 9am until 1pm. More business could be gathered in this time window than any other. Every industry is a little different on the specific time window. But let me assure you, your industry has a prime time.

If you sell into different industries then you may have multiple prime times, one for each industry. If you don't know what this is in the industry you work in, then find out quickly. When you figure it out, work hard to focus all your core activity into prime time.

Chronotype - Your Personal Prime Time

Personal prime time is the window when you are individually most awake, alert, and physically strong. My personal prime time matched up very closely with the industry prime time that I sold into. **To maximize effectiveness, so should yours. This time window is based on your own biological or circadian rhythms.** Are you a morning person or a night person? Are you a lark or an owl? Some people think they can go both ways. Maybe they can, but they might be fooling themselves. **You may be able to adjust it slightly by adjusting your bedtime** but on the whole, you are probably stuck with your unique personal prime time.

If you don't match up well, you should at least consider shifting into a career that better fits. If you are a hiring manager, ask questions about personal prime time when interviewing a new candidate. You want them to have every natural advantage possible when they first start out and hopefully continue for a long career.

I recommend a deeper dive on this topic. Read the book, *The Power of When*, by board certified sleep doctor Michael Breus. Start with his free chronotype assessment which you can find on the internet at thepowerofwhen.com. You will discover if your sleep patterns more closely resemble the lion, the bear, the dolphin or the wolf. Have each family member and everyone on your team take the quiz and then make appropriate adjustments to align with their natural chronotype. According to Dr. Mehmet Oz, who wrote the introduction, those adjustments could even save their life.

Your Main Event

Every day should have a main event or task, one that is more important than all the rest. Every week should have a main event or task as well. These high priority events, by some criteria, are more important to your success than the others in any given day or week.

For the most part, your main events should align heavily with your main strengths. They will be based on your highest passion and biggest talent. Your main event should consistently line up with your personal prime time.

If you are calling on an account that can produce $100,000 in sales and an account that can produce $10,000 in sales, you need to invest more preparation in the larger account. I once spent nearly a whole week preparing for a presentation to the largest account in my territory. The extra preparation paid off. We landed the account.

This is not an excuse to slack on service or preparation with the $10,000 account. It simply means extra preparation for the larger one.

Your main events should showcase your core strengths. Again, if there is a close match between your strengths and task/events, that will insure your success.

Your Windshield Time

How long is your commute? Maybe for you, it's in a carpool or your windshield is at the front of the subway train or airplane. For 8 years of my life, I was in and out of airplanes and airports. Most of us commute back and forth from our jobs. In outside sales, there is a "terrific" or "horrendous" amount of windshield time depending on your perspective. That is time we spend just sitting behind the wheel driving. The temptation is to use this to catch up on voicemail or phone calls. That's dangerous, so I have a hard time recommending it. If you do have a hands-free set, that may help, but doesn't eliminate all the danger.

I find driving to be a great time to think, plan, rehearse a call or presentation. I also use my automobile as a university or training center on wheels. I am constantly listening to recordings of educators, trainers and books while driving. I also keep all my *Apple* devices packed with inspirational music that helps keep me in a positive frame of mind. When the mind is not given direction, it can easily go negative.

Don't ever get gas in prime time. My first trainer and early manager was obsessed with this rule. Always try to complete simple mundane tasks when you are tired and can't be doing productive work. This may not seem like much, but little things add up. Get gas in non-prime time. If you drive a gas guzzler that is a waste of time also. Save time and the environment!

Your travel time can be maximized by viewing it through the lens of your strengths. The commute strategy can be intensely personal, but you should have one.

Fuel Your Routine

It has taken me a long time to learn about my unique body and its energy requirements. My first discovery, as a young teenager, was that milk chocolate gave me headaches, sometimes severe ones. I've also learned there is a strong correlation between lack of hydration, low energy and mental fatigue. I'm voraciously hungry around 4:30 everyday and need to make sure healthy food is close by to snack on.

Over the years, I've experimented with a number of eating strategies designed to maximize my energy level. My first plan was the *Fit or Fat Target Diet* taught by Covert Baily.

Currently, I'm using an Alkaline-Acid Balance strategy similar to the one promoted by Tony Robbins and his wife Sage. *New England Patriot* Quarterback, Tom Brady, also uses a version of this eating strategy that has been formulated by his trainer, Dr. Alex Guerrero. It is great for energy, weight loss/management and dramatically reduces inflammation related joint pain. I also incorporate intermittent fasting as recommend by Dr. Joseph Mercola.

Every body is different. In some cases, quite different. What works in one season of life may not work in another. My experience has been that my body changes about every 10 years and I have to dial in a new strategy. **If you're serious about maximizing your time, you'll invest the effort in figuring out what works for you in this season.**

A Bible passage I've been pondering is in chapter 4 of John's Gospel. Jesus was on a road trip with his team and apparently everyone was getting hungry... everyone but Jesus. I'm an all-day grazer and I'm with the disciples on this one. Jesus' response is so interesting. He tells them, "I have food you don't know about." If I'm with Jesus, I'm thinking he's got a candy bar stashed in his pack and didn't tell anyone. Like most of the stories about Jesus, the disciples are completely baffled. "Did someone bring him food?"

But that's not it. Jesus says, "My food is doing the will of God." Hmmm.... Have you ever had a made-for-this-moment, like you're doing what you were made to do? Is there an activity you do where you just know you're in alignment-with-your-assignment?

Did you get as hungry? Did you find yourself working through the morning break or even through the lunch hour and you're thinking where did the time go?

I'm convinced that at least **some** of the obesity problem in our country is really a result of work that doesn't fit. Eating that donut can just be task avoidance.

There are tasks and activities that will give you energy. Next time you reach for the donut, ask yourself, "Is God trying to tell me something? Am I in alignment with my assignment?"

Recharging

Arianna Huffington (founder, *Huffington Post Media Group*) says, "My single most effective trick for getting things done is to stop doing what I'm doing and get some sleep."

I keep a list of things that tend to recharge my batteries. I try to do some of them daily and most of them each weekend.

Malling - Shopping relaxes me… always has

Massage - I do 10 minutes at the mall because I'm cheap

Movies - Action and romantic comedies… you gotta laugh!!!!!

Meals - I love to eat at nice restaurants

Muscle Work Out - Some aerobics and strength training daily

Reading - Bible, business, personal growth, occasional novel

Bookstores – *Barnes & Noble*, used bookstores

Cafes - *Starbucks* and *Panera*

Friends - Phone, email, in person

Sammy – Giving my Labrador Retriever a belly scratch

Great Worship Service - Vibrant worship and inspiring message

Soaking – Special recordings of Scripture and music

Beaches - Everyday Susy and I are on the beach!

Work - Some work is self energizing … research, write, coach

Creativity - In business and ministry

Architecture & Art – Looking at great design
That's my list… make your own!

Your Morning Ritual

Phillip Johnson was one of the 20th century's premier architects. He designed some of America's most famous structures including the *Crystal Cathedral*; the *Seagram Building*, in collaboration with Mies van der Rohe; *Sculpture Garden* at the *Museum of Modern Art; New York State Theater at Lincoln Center; John F. Kennedy Memorial Plaza* in Dallas, Texas; *Boston Public Library* and dozens more projects not listed here.

He was once asked, "What is the most important part of a building?" His answer, "The Goesinto … That part of the building you enter through."

Well begun is half done. The most important part of a trip into space is **the launch.** The most important part of a speech is **the beginning**. My younger years were filled with bad starts. I had a lot of problem with my shirts and the buttons being misaligned. Finally I figured out that if I got that first button in the right button hole, the other buttons pretty well took care of themselves. Time management is a lot like that.

People Management International founder Arthur F. Miller Jr. says, "Your agenda will be driven by your design. Not only will you focus on what you value most, you'll avoid things that hold little motivational value for you, or the things you don't do well. What happens when a person possessing a certain giftedness approaches each day? A typical scenario would be that when one wakes up in the morning, one starts thinking about some person or problem or situation of motivational interest."

I agree! If you are in work that is well aligned to who you are, you will immediately begin thinking about your dreams, directions and destinations. Those visions will wake you up and put you to sleep. But if you're not naturally aligned with your work, those waking thoughts may turn to dreads, dark tunnels and dead ends.

I recommend crafting a morning ritual at the beginning of your routine. I have varied my morning ritual over the years, but for the most part I've always had one. More on this later under the segment on *Eating Frogs*. In general, I'm a big believer that the first steps of your day should be magnetic, compelling and something you look forward to immensely.

My current routine is:

½ hour snuggling Susy and listening to *NPR* news
Get up, turn on the *MacBook Pro*
Grind coffee beans and brew
Turn on worship music
Check email
Open current writing project
Shave and shower
Bible reading with Susy
Walk on the beach
Dress
Work (Hopefully Writing)

I have a night ritual as well. I try to change things up once in while, but **I believe the right ritual, one that is**

deeply connected to your passion, talent and values will dramatically improve your productive use of time.

Your Ideal Day
"Choose a path that lets you be extraordinary."
~Vishen Lakhiani

Pull all of these strengths, destinations, signature routes and routines together. Get crystal clear on your strengths, letting them point you toward a set of signature targets. Then build a route and routine, which if repeated, will get you quickly to your signature destinations and offer a great time along the way.

For many people it may make sense to build an ideal day or route, before settling in on the destinations. More goal setting heresy, I know. At the end of the day, your strengths are all about activities you do best, enjoy and that create value for others.

Experiment with assembling your ideal day of activities and then figure out where those activities will lead. Then set up your targets. Some career counselors recommend assembling an ideal day as a method for selecting your profession. I agree.

Always do the highest payoff activity available to you. Ruthlessly pull low payoff activities or rearrange them to non prime time. By the way, breaks, lunch, and even 20 minute power naps are <u>not</u> low payoff activities. You need them to reflect and restore. Just don't kid yourself and overdo it. In the long run, low-talent, low-passion activities are almost always low payoff.

When I think about putting together an ideal day, I think about content. What are the tasks and activities that deliver your passion and talent in ways that add value? But part of the equation is the length of your work day and the work type segments within the day.

I recently read that any work over 25 hours a week causes brain damage for those over 40 years of age. That may be true if you are working way outside your zone of strengths. For those working in the passion and talent zones, I believe your work should radically enhance your brain development.

Still, there will be significant individual differences. As President, Jimmy Carter worked long days as did President Clinton. Ronald Reagan famously was an 8 to 5 guy who napped during cabinet meetings. Reagan joked, "I know hard work never killed anybody but why take the risk?" The point is, if you want to optimize your day, you will need to work out the specific details based on a number of factors.

Exponential Results

Let's review! As I mentioned in the introduction, the suggestions in this book don't all have equal value. The ideas won't give you the same amount of progress. To borrow from the language of Stephen Covey, there are 3 big rocks in strengths based time management. Once those are placed, the smaller, less important rocks can then be inserted around them:

Strengths – Discovering, Developing and Delivering your passion, talent, personality and values in a way that makes increasingly bigger contributions is the first big rock.

Nothing is a bigger time waster than consistently working from weakness.

Targets – Working on the signature Dreams, Vision and Goals that flow from your strengths is the second big rock. Strengths and target disconnect is the single greatest cause of low achievement.

Routes – Using your strengths to reach your targets while on your signature path is the third big rock of strengths based time management. There is a strategy that is designed just for you. It will leverage your signature strengths and will accelerate your progress dramatically.

These 3 rocks will bring you exponential results and accelerate your achievement beyond anything else you can personally do. They will cause you to grow and succeed dramatically! Exponential means by a factor of 10, that is 10x better, bigger, faster. That's what the first three chapters of this book has focused on.

Incremental Results

Don't overlook incremental time management progress. Incremental improvement is what the Japanese call Kaizen. The *Toyota Motor Company* reports that they **implement** one million improvements in productivity each year. This adds up to huge gains. The rest of this book will be devoted to some ideas and methods that will help you manage your time better, incrementally.

Just remember, your exponential gains will come about as you get in alignment and stay in alignment with your God-given passions and talents. Once the exponential gains are consistently made, then move on to the incremental ones. My mom uses an old saying. It comes from the words of

Jesus in the Gospel of Matthew that says, "You strained at a gnat and swallowed a camel." It means you got all excited about the little things and missed the main thing. This is easy to do in time management. It's easy to do with anything. You can run all over looking for the best calendar and keep the best to-do list, but if you're not working from signature strengths, moving toward signature destinations and taking signature routes, you won't be maximizing your time.

CHAPTER 4

Classic Time Management...
Revised

Most time management books were written in the last century and based on a false premise – that you can be good at anything. But this time management book is based on your unique strengths. It begins with your signature strengths, moves to your signature targets or destinations and then to your signature routes. In this section, we'll review some of the best ideas from time management experts of the last century. And I will encourage you to adapt or reinvent them with a focus around your signature strengths.

Lakein's Question

Former U.S. President Bill Clinton started his autobiography, *My Life*, with a reference to a book. He wrote, "When I was a young man just out of law school and eager to get on with my life, on a whim I briefly put aside my reading preference for fiction and history and bought one of those how-to books: *How to Get Control of Your Time and Your Life*, by Alan Lakein. I still have that paperback book, now almost thirty years old." This book, referenced by former President Clinton is probably the classic book of all time on time management.

I have several "different" hobbies. I love to read, visit bookstores and build my library. I collect training props and comic strips. I also collect interesting questions. Some I use to engage other people and others I use for personal reflection. One of my favorite all-time questions was crafted by Alan Lakein and offered as a foundational point in his book.

Lakein's Question is simple... "What's the best use of my time right now?" He recommends asking this several times throughout the day. I have this one pretty well stamped on my brain. It gets me to a sense of priorities faster than almost anything I can think of.

I picked up a complimentary idea from the manager of a *New York Life Insurance* office in 1979 while on a sales call. I noticed a 1/8" red dot... the kind you can get at any office supply store very inexpensively. The manager had fixed it to the face of his watch. Every time he looked at his watch, it would remind him to ask Lakein's Question. Give it a try. It's always time to use your time well.

In his book *18 Minutes*, Peter Bregman shares the strategy of setting his watch to beep every hour. When he hears the chime, he asks himself if the last hour has been productive and makes a commitment for the next hour.

We can build on either Lakein's or Bregman's Question by adding the strengths component. Regularly ask yourself, "Am I making the best use of my time by using my strengths?" If you are consistently working from weakness, you're not using your time well.

Implement the red dot or beep strategy. If you don't wear a watch, use your mobile device. Remind yourself to ask a specific strengths based productivity question.

The $25K Idea

It's hard to imagine a time management strategy much more classic than the to-do list. But successful people differ.

Virgin founder Richard Branson says, "I have always lived my life by making lists: lists of people to call, lists of ideas, lists of companies to set up, lists of people who can make things happen. Each day I work through these lists, and that sequence of calls propels me forward."

Microsoft founder Bill Gates says, "I'm not big on to-do lists. Instead, I use email and desktop folders and my online calendar. So when I walk up to my desk, I can focus on the emails I've flagged and check the folders that are monitoring particular projects and particular blogs."

In the early 1900's Charles M. Schwab, who was then President of *Bethlehem Steel*, called in management consultant Ivy Lee to spend some time observing the company executives and recommend ways to increase productivity. After careful analysis, Lee sent along a single idea with the request to have the executives try it out and then send a check for whatever Schwab felt it was worth. Lee's idea? Every morning write down on a piece of paper the 6 most important things to do that day. Start with the most important first, take it to completion and then move on to the next. After a fair trial, Schwab sent Lee a check for $25,000.00. Schwab later claimed this one simple idea helped him make millions.

Living a day without a well-thought-out list is like sitting down to the piano and randomly playing notes with no thought to order, balance, contrast, unity, and harmony. The results are jumbled, chaotic and discordant. It's okay to improvise, but improvisation implies a base plan. Max Depree writes in *Leadership Jazz*, "I find that a list brings a sort of discipline to my thinking and I look at a good list as a musical score – Before it really comes to life it must be interpreted and performed."

Richard Lieder writes in *Life Skills*, "When you stop and think about it, everyone relies on lists. They're useful. They save time. They inspire fantasies. They get results."

Finally Robert Schuller writes, "We all need lists! When we have no projects, no causes, no issues, no concerns, no dreams, we become listless, which is just one stage above depression. We need an 'I – would – like – to– do' list. We need an 'I – wish– I – could – do' list. We need a 'wouldn't – it – be – fantastic?' list. Look at your list of possibilities everyday and everyday you'll be enthused. <u>If you're listless – it could be because you're list-less!</u>"

It seems to me, in spite of what he said, Bill Gates does make lists, they are just formatted electronically by file folders. There are now a plethora of electronic options. Three of my favorites are *I Done This, Trello* and *Evernote.* They can be easily shared electronically and these tools can be pulled up on your smart phone or tablet. I keep my strengths list there and sometimes review my to-do list for how many are connected to my strengths. 3x5 cards are old school, but a format I still use.

Calendar – Clock – Compass - Banana

There are a variety of time devices that have been used through history. In the Malay and Tamil languages around Indonesia there is a phrase, *pisan zapra or pisang zapra*. The grammar of the phrase apparently adds a time dimension which roughly translates the phrase to mean, "About the time it takes to eat a banana." When I first read this, I immediately had an image of Malaysian peoples walking around with a banana strapped to their wrist. I'm guessing this referred to a short period of time, something like our 60 seconds.

Clocks have only been a relevant time device since the 1850's when the cost began to come down. In a mostly agricultural economy, the sunrise, sunset and seasons of a year were the main time markers. With the industrial revolution came the obsession with working by the clock, the hourly wage and happy hour.

Timers like the hour glass are thought to have been invented in Alexandria, around 150 B.C. The *Pomodoro Time Management Strategy* makes use of 25 minute productivity sprints. It was developed in the early 1990's by software developer Francesco Cirillo who tracked his university work with a tomato shaped timer. When faced with a large task or series of tasks he broke them down into 25 minute *Pomodoro Productivity Sprints*. Each sprint was interspersed with 5 minute breaks and a longer break after 4 sprints. The system trains your brain to focus while increasing concentration and attention span. The strategy can be easily combined with the *Agile* program discussed in chapter 9.

Stopwatches are mostly used in athletic practice and events but they do sometimes creep into the workplace.

Time and motion studies have their place at work and can lead to improved productivity and efficiency. Keyboard speed is a great contemporary example. To test yours and improve, go to type-test.com.

The ancient Romans are believed to have invented the calendar or at least came up with the word – calendarium, which means register. A calendar is a place to register or keep track of appointments and commitments. Your schedule of events belong on a calendar. Usually your events can be assigned to a specific day for a specific time and a specific duration. This allows you to pack your days and weeks efficiently. You want your day loaded fairly tight but not too tight. If you are jammed too tight and something runs over, you will start getting behind on appointments and being late for other commitments.

Some are still using paper calendars, but the *Google* calendar is hard to beat. Again, it's easy to share.

I once read that Bill Gates has an associate review his calendar periodically and make suggestions on how to be more effective. This is potentially a great productivity boosting idea, especially if the reviewer deeply understands strengths and weaknesses. The calendar must be reviewed for how well the schedule matches innate strengths. I **recommend scheduling your strengths!** Put them on a calendar. I also recommend hiring a strengths strategist to help with this review when you're getting started. Begin with a weekly review and over a few months, move your reviews farther apart as you learn to manage your strengths with regard to time. Eventually move to monthly reviews and then quarterly.

The compass seems more like a directional device than a time device. But time and direction should be linked. Stephen Covey once advised his daughter, a new mother at the time, to temporarily drop all of the clocks and calendars and productivity devices she had brought over from the workplace. Covey advised her to replace them with a metaphorical compass, a tool much more suited to maximizing time with her newborn baby.

Susy and I just spent 5 days caring for our new granddaughter. I agree with Covey. Clocks and calendars aren't well suited for a 4 month old and the adults that care for them.

The overall life lesson is to be aware of your time tools. Don't assume that one tool will work equally well across all work events and platforms. Always consider the individual situation as well as the unique strengths and preferences of the people involved.

Schedules and Structures

Schedules are pre-determined structures of how you will spend your time. David Allen teaches that there are 3 types of work:

- Planning or pre-determining your work
- Doing planned or pre-determined work
- Doing work as it comes in

Most time management trainers would probably insist that the best use of time is to stick closely with the first two bullet points. This is often true, but not always. Sometimes an opportunity or problem walks through your door that trumps the schedule.

I've read that Barak Obama keeps to a strict schedule. The President reportedly insists on his morning workout, dinner with his daughters, and having a late night block of time devoted to reading and preparing for the next day's work. But I'm pretty confident that when a big opportunity or big problem shows up, he changes the schedule.

If you always stick with your schedule, you may have a rigidity problem. If you are always deviating, you may have a discipline problem.

Some structures or schedules come prepackaged off the shelf. A good example is Tony Horton's *P90X* exercise program. It structures an hour of your day for 90 days. Another example is a Read-Through-The-Bible-In-A-Year program.

If you are regularly deviating from your schedule, that may be a sign of task avoidance and that you are consistently scheduling work that isn't on your *STRENGTHSPATH.*

Priorities

Most time management systems talk about prioritizing activities, but few if any, start with the importance of prioritizing your unique strengths. Everyone should put together a prioritized list of their top strengths. Keep a list of the 3 or 4 activities you are best at in front of you until it's in your bones.

I recommend starting by prioritizing your strengths beginning with your passion, moving to your talents and then values. Your passions will get you on topic and in the right arena. Your talents will get you on task doing what you're made to do. Your values will get you in the right organization and on the right team.

Once you're in a specific role, you must get very clear on the core payoff activity and activate all of your strengths on that task. If your passion and talent based activities don't have sufficient impact on the core activity, you're either in the wrong job or you haven't learned to leverage your strengths.

The 80/20 Rule

A lot of space has been given in time management books to the 80/20 Rule based on the concepts of Vilfredo Paretto, a 19th century Italian economist. The business ramifications of the principle were described by quality consultant Joseph Juran in the 1950's. Juran, who worked in the post World War II rebuilding of Japan, is largely responsible for the surge of quality in Japanese cars. He proposed that quality issues could be eliminated most effectively by focusing on the 20% that were causing 80% of the problems.

Time management strategist Jim Koch has written several time management books and programs just amplifying and applying this one idea in different ways. As a primer, I recommend his book, *The 80/20 Principle*.

In a nutshell, applied to time management, the 80/20 Rule says, "80% of your results come from 20% of your activities." Put another way - If you perform 10 activities in your work role, 2 of those activities will account for the majority of your positive results. 80% of your outputs come from 20% of your inputs. 80% of consequences come from 20% of causes. 20% of efforts are responsible for 80% of results. If you have 10 products, 80% of the sales will come from 2 of them. If you have 10 customers, 80% of your sales will come from 2 of them. Go look in your closet. You wear 20% of your clothes 80% of the time. 20% of your carpet will get 80% of the wear.

More significantly for our topic of strengths based time management, 80% of your sales will come from 20% of your sales representatives. Out of 10 representatives, the top 2 will bring in more revenue than the other 8 combined. Why? Because they are more talented and work with more passion.

This is essentially why Jack Welch, who is a big advocate of the strengths philosophy, had *General Electric* close or sell every business unit that wasn't number one or number two in the market place. It's also why his employee *Topgrading System* that required sorting each employee by performance level was so effective.

Where are you ineffective? Where do you need to fire or re-position yourself? Give yourself a nice severance package, a gold watch and let yourself go.

Who are the employees you need to reposition so they can be successful and work in their strengths? If you don't have a position that fits, come up with the most generous severance package you can, offer outplacement help and take all the responsibility for the hiring mistake.

Put together an ongoing *Full-Throttle* recruiting program that is focused on hiring those rare top performers who will drive the success of your business unit.

Multi-Tasking?

Time management tactics go in and out of style. Currently, multi-tasking is out of style and focused single tasking is in. There is research on this, showing that true multi-tasking doesn't exist. Some analysts say it's actually just rapid task shifting. There is even research suggesting it damages the brain.

I think this is situational and clearly a strengths issue. Should you multi-task or single task? My answer is yes... you should probably do both depending on your talents, skills and experience level.

Do you drive a stick? Do you clutch and move the gear shift, work the accelerator, steer, look in the rearview mirror and stay aware of what's in front of you?

Have you ever watched a skilled guitarist hold a chord while strumming? Have you ever seen a guitarist play the harmonica simultaneously?

How about the piano? Have you seen a right and left hand playing different parts?

How about the drums? Have you seen a skilled drummer play double bass drums, snare, hi-hat and ride cymbal all at once?

Do you read? How many of you read one letter at a time? Do you read and recognize groups of letters called words and groups of words called phrases and sentences, all at a glance?

Skilled martial artists learn to deliver multiple strikes simultaneously.

Former financier and philanthropist Michael Milken reportedly read while driving. I hope he's stopped that.

J. Willard Marriot Sr. reportedly went to workshops taking notes simultaneously with both hands. With one hand he would write down ideas and the other he would write down actions he wanted to take.

Turnaround king, *Gap* and *J. Crew* CEO, Mickey Drexler starts his day making phone calls while on the treadmill. I've done this and just about wiped out a few times. Proceed with caution.

Multi-Pathing

In his *Nightingale-Conant* audio program, *Dreams Don't Have Deadlines*, Mark Victor Hansen talks about the benefits of multipathing. He described his visit with the late Steve Allen, a comedian/author/song writer who wrote 53 books and 8500 songs during his career. Allen kept 28 different recorders near his desk. When he got stuck on one song, he moved on to another. Hansen also described a plane trip with a close associate of Bill Gates. The *Microsoft* employee said Gates had 1610 projects at the time.

Multi-Purposing

Some activities can be arranged to accomplish several goals simultaneously. Susy and I walk on the beach every single morning. This is a time for us to connect as partners. We do this right after our Bible reading and discuss the passage on our walk. This helps us grow spiritually as individuals and also sync up with God and each other. We wear our *Fitbits* and get a good start on our daily 10,000 steps. Our walk is part of our fitness and weight management strategy. The walk is a great stress reducer. We also pick up broken glass and trash each morning. We are doing our part for the environment, animals and protecting the bare feet of young children. On our most productive walk, we picked up 446 pieces of glass. We are helping drive the tourist based local economy who prefer to visit safe, clean beaches. Susy and I also engage with other regular beach walkers and their dogs. We've gotten to know Ozzie, Mindy, Annie, Chika, April, Domingo, Killer, Nellie and their humans as well. This single activity leverages our strengths, moves us in the direction of signature goals while traveling on our signature routes. That's a lot to get accomplished in less than a single hour each day. It starts us off with a sense of connection, shared mission and sets us up emotionally for more productivity, engagement and satisfaction. You don't have to live on the beach to do this. We started the habit before we moved to paradise.

I've dabbled in several martial arts over the years. I've always been fascinated by the applications that each has had outside of self-defense. One of my favorites was *American Kenpo*, developed by Ed Parker. It's an extremely cerebral art with a lot of strategy. One of the principles of *Kenpo* is that every single move has multiple purposes. Every blocking action is also a cocking action that prepares for a strike. Grafting is a concept that combines several principles within the flow of a single action. Marriage of gravity combines the force of a strike with a dropping motion adding power.

Almost any single activity can accomplish multiple purposes if you organize it that way. You can utilize other people to get tasks accomplished. Certainly that's part of what a manager does. Even more importantly, if you organize it correctly, you can utilize a task to build a person. You can help them develop and grow. You can also set the task up in ways that help them discover, develop and deliver their strengths. You can make a task more enjoyable and teach people how to make work fun. Borrowing from our beach walk, make your meetings move. Go for a walk. People are less intimidated on walk-a-longs. They open up and get some exercise. Energy levels are raised in the short-term and weight is lost in the long-term. Any activity can be multi-purposed and leveraged toward multiple goals. But only if you set it up that way.

Action

"The path to success is to take massive determined action."
~Tony Robbins

In a very real sense, time management is actually action management. You don't really manage time, it just keeps moving along doing its thing. Time management is managing action with regard to time. It's taking **more action**, taking **better action** and taking **action better**. This is the time management triangle and it's at the core.

In the beginning of any new activity, I often recommend a simple focus on taking more action. Throw more mud against the walls and see what sticks. Then I recommend experimenting with walls. Change walls. See if the mud sticks better on one wall surface than another. And lastly, improve your mud throwing motion. Try right hand, left hand, underhand, overhand and ¾ side arm. See what gets the best results.

This was the foundation of all the sales training I did. Whenever I worked with a rep, I would ask about their activity level and try to determine how many potential clients they were approaching on a daily/weekly basis. Then I would look at what type of potential client they were focused on. Were they qualified based on the size of the organization or was there some wheel spinning going on there? Finally, I looked at sales sequence. How effective were they in the different parts of the sales presentation process?

I can't imagine a business or type of work that this doesn't apply to. If you are a writer, teacher, athlete, artist, minister, doctor, lawyer, carpenter or plumber, this time triangle applies.

1. Do you need to take more action?
2. Do you need to take better action?
3. Do you need to take action better?

Of the three approaches, which comes more naturally to you? Number three is my strength, followed by number two and then number one.

If you are avoiding action, it's almost always because the particular type of action you're avoiding is outside your strengths set. The ignored activity doesn't reflect your passion, talent, personality or values.

One contribution of a good coach is to help you "forward the action". But a good strengths coach will help you engage with the actions that best align with your natural abilities. He or she will also help you tweak your approaches for better alignment.

Think!

"Follow effective action with quiet reflection. From quiet reflection will come more effective action."
~Peter Drucker

Thinking is a form of action. Sara Blakely is the founder of *Spanx* and the world's first self-made female billionaire. Sara says that thinking is a hobby for her. Every morning, before heading to her office which is only a few blocks from her home, she drives around the highway 285 Atlanta Beltway... just to think. One recent study showed this highway to be the most dangerous in the nation with 2,867 fatalities in 2013. Maybe she is a bit of a daredevil as well.

Ford Motor Company founder, Henry Ford once hired a consultant to walk the floors of his organization and look for ways to improve productivity. The consultant reported back that everything looked good with the exception of one man, who the consultant found sitting and thinking with his feet up on the desk. Ford responded, "That man is the most important person in our organization. I pay him to do nothing but sit and think."

B.C. Forbes came to America in 1904, acquired a job as a newspaper reporter and went on to start *Forbes Magazine* in 1917. He was planning to call the magazine *Doers and Doings* but friends convinced him to use his own name. Forbes was a man of action. But one of his most important writings was titled, *In Budgeting Your Days – Allow Time for Thinking*. Forbes wrote about Ned Harriman, the railroad wizard who once declared that he liked to drop in unannounced and find one of his executives with his feet up on the desk, apparently doing nothing. Harriman assumed that the man was taking his time to think.

Forbes wrote, "Isn't it true that nine executives of every ten would hesitate, would be almost ashamed to be seen sitting at a desk apparently completely idle? Has it not become fashionable to appear busy?" He continued, "Do we always keep in mind the simple, basic fact that all success springs from thinking? Not only success but everything else comes into being as a thought in some man's mind. The *Woolworth Building* for years was nothing more than a thought, an idea, in the mind of Frank W. Woolworth. The billion-dollar *Steel Corporation* first was thought in the mind of one individual, generally understood to have been Charles M. Schwab. If we can only get it firmly in our heads, and will eternally keep it in the forefront of our mind, that thinking is the material of which success is made, will it not influence us to so plan our days and our weeks that we shall set aside more time for calm, sustained thinking?"

Long-time *IBM* chief Thomas Watson, had a sign over his office desk that simply said, "Think!". Watson wrote, "All the problems of the world could be settled easily if men were only willing to think. The trouble is that men very often resort to all sorts of devices in order not to think, because thinking is such hard work." Watson encouraged everyone to be a thinker including assembly line workers, secretaries and salespeople. The word "Think!" which was to become the *IBM* company slogan, got started at a managers meeting in 1911. The managers weren't able to come up with any ideas on how to improve the company. Watson told them, "Knowledge is a result of thought, and thought is the keynote of success in this and any business." "Think!" got posted on walls in every *IBM* office. The employee magazine was titled *Think!*, notebooks were handed out with the word "Think!" embossed on the cover.

John Maxwell says he used to refer to thinking as if it were a single skill. Today, he describes it as a mental decathlon with at least 10 events. Maxwell has actually written on 11 of them including: "Big Picture, Focused, Creative, Realistic,

Strategic, Possibility, Reflective, Questioning, Shared, Unselfish and Bottom-Line Thinking."

Great coaches help clients deepen their learning. The essence of a reflective practice is asking the question, "Is what you're doing making a difference? Is it having the intended result? Are there destructive unintended consequences? Are there better ways? Are there ways that fit you better?" Great strengths coaches help clients think about their strengths, their most naturally effective actions and connect the dots.

Time Boxing

I said in my first words of the prologue, "Time is an unstoppable sequence of events. I tend to think of those events as different size boxes or nesting containers." *Wikipedia* says, "Time boxing allocates a fixed **time** period, called a **time box**, to each planned activity." Although I've never participated, I'm told speed dating is known for its 7 minute time boxes. *Ted Talks* work with a 20 minute speech time frame. The time management strategy I referred to earlier as *Pomodoro*, uses 25 minute time boxes.

Time boxing is an accent to scheduling tasks that don't necessarily involve commitments and appointments with other people. You might think of a time box as an appointment with yourself, although it can have group applications as with a 21 day Sprint in *Agile Project Management*.

The essence of a time box is performing a very specific task for a very specific period of time. Time boxing may also involve grouping task types. You might group errands by area of town, for example. I often group my work by what I call **Hat Style**. It's based on my grandmother's admonition to, "Put On Your Thinking Cap". I found a long time ago that I don't easily shift back and forth between types of tasks. By grouping tasks that are highly active or highly reflective, I'm better at each. After working at a particular kind of task for an extended period, I suffer burnout and need to switch. I find continuing through burnout delivers diminishing returns. I don't believe there are any universal rules of thumb for time frames or what works. You'll need to experiment.

Time boxing really is a cornerstone to effective time management. By putting the boxes on a calendar, it allows you to reflect on the effectiveness of those activities. That's the essence of an *Agile* Sprint Review in chapter 8. By reflecting on our strengths at that time, we can consider both team strengths and individual strengths and make adjustments and improvements for the future.

Time Traps

R. Alec Mackenzie wrote several books identifying time traps that individuals in different roles face. The traps are position specific and I recommend that you spend a few weeks creating your own list of time traps.

Some of the traps on Mackenzie's list include: paperwork, red tape, ineffective delegation, telephone interruptions, disorganization, lack of self-discipline, attempting too much, inadequate goal setting, inadequate planning, crisis management, procrastination, drop-in visitors, un-necessary meetings, ineffective meetings, travel, incomplete information, inadequate staff, confused authority channels, inability to say no, excessive socializing, inadequate tools and poor filing systems.

These time traps can be huge wasters of time and resources. But to be accurately assessed, they must be viewed through the lens of individual strengths.

The biggest time trap you face is regularly engaging in work outside of your natural strengths. The second trap is working on goals that are disconnected from your strengths or otherwise don't fit you. The third trap is establishing routes and routines that don't optimize your gifts.

Once you've done some work aligning those 3 areas, look at Mackenzie's lists found in his books and resources. Go through each of the traps he discusses and add to these based on your own experience. Then make adjustments. Your signature strengths, goals and routes will give you a baseline to work from.

Deskmanship

Andrew DuBrin, an industrial psychologist at the *Rochester Institute of Technology* has accurately noted, "Whenever you see a photo of a powerful person, the person always has a clean work area." DuBrin's observation is spot on. In our Northern European culture, the failure to keep a neat desk suggests character issues or at least questions about competency.

When I was growing up, my dad would come home with stories about his boss, Jim Cox. He headed the construction company where my dad worked before starting his own. Jim kept an impeccably clean desk and left everyday at 5pm. My dad succeeded in numerous business ventures, but for the most part, a clean desk and 8 to 5 hours eluded him.

In an interview with Eugene Griessman, Bill Marriott shared a secret about his dad, J. Willard Marriott Sr., founder of the hotel chains. Bill said, "My father always believed in having a clean desk. One day we discovered the way he had a clean desk was to dump everything in a drawer."

I worked for 16 years in the *Olan Mills* organization and had the opportunity of visiting Mr. Mills' office. He kept two offices. The outer office was opulent, immaculate and designed for meetings and receiving guests. On one occasion, I got inside his working office. Chaos! Books and papers everywhere. When I subsequently purchased my first new house, I remembered and arranged a similar set up. It was a brilliant solution. In the outer office, I could look smart by all the cultural standards and then work effectively in my inner sanctum.

Tom Peters has written many incredibly helpful business books. One was titled, *Thriving On Chaos*. People in some positions do just that. Dee Hock, the founder of *Visa*, coined a word that immediately resonated with me..."Chaordic". It's the blend of chaos and order.

Albert Einstein, sported one of the messiest work environments one could imagine and yet he was one of the best thinkers in history. In their book, *A Perfect Mess*, Eric Abrahamson and David H. Freedman argue that a messy desk can be an attribute of an effective worker. They offer compelling research along with many examples other than Einstein.

I'm not trying to make a case for working in a mess. My point is that the whole matter is an issue of individual strengths. Some people work more effectively from chaos, some a chaordic blend and others from perfect order. I would also add that cutting edge science suggests that what looks like chaos on the surface is very ordered underneath.

Discipline

What is the role of discipline in strengths based career development? This is really a crux-of-the-matter question. A high percentage of us find ourselves in jobs where the tasks we're good at and enjoy, are not what we're hired to do.

As Steve Jobs reminded us, success is really hard. Working in our passions while applying our talents, doesn't remove hard work. I love to write and I've been at it here for the last 5 hours with almost no breaks. My legs are about to cramp and my brain is getting close to being fried. But I love it. I have a certain talent for doing research and arranging thoughts on paper. I'm working on improving the skill dimension. My wife helps with grammar, spelling and an occasional content adjustment for better communication. It's hard work. But it's hard work I love. There is a certain discipline about it, or as Vishen Lakhiani calls it, *Blissipline*.

Next, there is the discipline of staying in your strengths. The insistence on working in your strengths is still very much a counter-cultural revolutionary act in some circles. The lazy misinformed mantra in both the classroom and the boardroom is that, "Anyone can do anything. If you're not successful, you're just not working at it." Part of my mission is to change that.

Also, there is the discipline of doing tasks that are clearly out of our strengths zone. The transition to a strengths based life is a work in progress. Bill Hendricks has been working for a couple of decades helping others make strengths based career transitions. He's worked with thousands of clients and estimates it takes 5 to 7 years to make a complete transition. There will be disappointments, defeats and setbacks just like any other area of life.

Procrastination

There is more than one way to look at procrastination through the lens of strengths. *Wharton Business School* professor Adam Grant suggests that while procrastination is a liability in production work, it can be an asset in creative work. He sites Leonardo da Vinci and architect Frank Lloyd Wright as two famous procrastinators. Leonardo put off finishing the *Mona Lisa* for years and Wright put off beginning his *Falling Water* design for months. I keep a *Lego* version of the latter on my desk as a reminder.

Jessica Hische is an American letterer, illustrator, and type designer. She wisely writes, **"The work you do while you procrastinate is probably the work you should be doing for the rest of your life."** This is the best insight I've ever heard on procrastination. When you're not working on what you're "supposed to be working on", what is it you do?

What is the work you do when you're procrastinating? That's probably something close to what God put you on the planet to work on. What do you keep gravitating towards? What keeps pulling you back? This is a great place to look for career guidance. Some version of this topic or task has probably been pulling at you since you were a child.

In my case, I was pretty good at writing papers in school. I still remember my first speech in 6th grade and it was a very positive experience. When I was working as a contractor, I kept my shirt pocket full of 3x5 cards. I'd scribble down notes for writing as I worked on construction projects. I couldn't help it. I had to get the ideas out of my head and onto paper. I still have some of those cards 30 years later and that information is part of this book.

So my first advice on procrastination is to look at it as a huge potential message from God about what you're really supposed to be doing with your life. But don't quit your day job. As I said in the last chapter, there may be a multi-year transitional process ahead.

Career coach Christine Mims talks about what she calls, "Passion Clumps". She writes, "Passion clumps is the idea that finding your passion and building a fulfilling career is rarely a short and linear experience. Instead, you do some stuff, think about some stuff, get angry or frustrated about other stuff, do more stuff again, and the insight comes *in bursts over time, with effort.* In other words, progress to your passion happens most often in clumps." This is such a brilliantly accurate description of career transitions. They are often messy. Her role, as well as mine, is to speed up the clumpiness and get you into the career that fits faster.

There will be times that you're procrastinating and you just need to get it done. Time management expert Alan Lakein recommends when you are having trouble putting off a high priority task, commit to doing nothing until and unless you begin that task. Give it a try.

On his uber popular website *43folders*, Merlin Mann suggests a *SUCCESSPATH* Math technique he calls (10+2)*5. It's 10 minute work boxes, 2 minute break boxes, repeated 5 times. Try it.

Eating Frogs?

"If you've got a frog to swallow, don't look at him too long. If you've got two frogs to swallow, eat the biggest one first." This phrase has been used by motivational speakers since Mark Twain and I'm sure goes back much further. Brian

Tracy has been one of my favorite authors and speakers for years. He has written an entire book, *Eat That Frog*, expounding on the topic.

It simply means, if you have an extremely difficult task in any given day, get it out of the way. Do it the first thing. If you've got two difficult tasks, do the hardest one first. It's terrific advice and everyone should have this technique in their playbook. The problem comes when 50% or even 80% of your job is swallowing frogs. The other problem is failing to recognize that one person's frog is another person's filet mignon. Albert Gray gave a speech in 1940 that was turned into a very popular motivational booklet, *The Common Denominator of Success*. Gray's central thesis was, "The secret of success for every man who has ever been successful --- lies in the fact that he formed the habit of doing things that failures don't like to do." Gray's speech was given to life insurance salespeople and specifically referred to contacting strangers to make a sale. This idea has been used to encourage salespeople of all stripes, motivating them to do an activity that many detest. I've personally made tens of thousands of these sales calls. I was actually fairly good at it. Over time, I was able to piece together a method that was fairly effective and tolerable. But for the most part, I hated doing it. And I'm convinced there are people who are both good at it and enjoy doing it. They would have been a better hire than I was. If grit and discipline is pushing you through the core activity of your day, you're not in the job God designed you for.

Chapter 10 of Brian Tracy's, *Eat That Frog*, is titled *Leverage Your Special Talents*. He writes, "Successful people are invariably those who have taken the time to identify what they do well and most enjoy. They know what they do that really makes a difference in their work, and then concentrate on that task or area exclusively." To his credit, Brian has incorporated the strengths message into most everything he writes now. My fear is that research shows most people only read the first 50 pages of a book. However, the strength message in *Eat That Frog* comes on page 59.

There is an educational version of "Frog Eating" that is driving our dropout rates sky high. According to college professor Andrew Hacker, higher mathematics is the biggest frog behind the statistics. Kids don't quit things they enjoy and are good at. The "grit glorifiers" and "math messiahs" need to stop. I'm not opposed to making our kids suffer. I just want them to suffer at something they enjoy and are good at.

My advice is to figure out the task that is both someone else's frog and your filet mignon. Do something that many people hate or don't have time for and you love. You will make bank and laugh all the way there!

Momentum

Facebook founder, Mark Zuckerberg offers an alternative to the Frog Eating philosophy in the previous section when he says, **"I think a simple rule of business is, if you do the things that are easier first, then you can actually make a lot of progress."** This is upside down to what classic time management trainers have taught for decades. What if they have been wrong all along? Maybe you need a Frog Eating day now and then. But what if Zuckerberg is right? Honestly, I don't see super successful people eating a lot of frogs. Warren Buffett is tap dancing to work every morning.

In *The 21 Irrefutable Laws of Leadership*, John Maxwell talks about the value of Momentum. As he describes it, "Momentum is the leader's best friend. Momentum is the great exaggerator. It makes you better than you are". Of course it's everyone's best friend. It makes us all better than we are. Whenever I took over a losing business unit, my first goal was to establish positive momentum. My mantra was, Get Stopped, Get Stable, Get Successful, Get Soaring. Once you're soaring, the amount of effort required is greatly reduced.

There is no bigger daily momentum buster than waking up with a sense of dread. There's nothing worse than walking into the office and having that ugly frog greet you at the door.

Remember, that ugly frog is a task that someone else would love to have greet them at the door. If you're consistently hitting the snooze button, you've got a frog problem. And you're robbing someone else of a delightful opportunity.

In his book *The Ultimate Power*, Dave Grant talked about, "The power of I can hardly wait". If you're a business owner, make sure the first task each employee does in the morning is something they look forward to. Attendance will improve. Tardiness will decrease. Sick days will disappear. Numerous *Gallup* studies prove this.

A lot of motivational speakers have gone around the country saying, "You've got to pay the price for success." As Zig Ziglar said, "You pay the price for failure...You enjoy the price of success." And I would add... You need to enjoy the process. All of the most successful people enjoy the process.

I'm not a motivational author or speaker. I'm a trainer and coach who will help you discover, develop and deliver your own authentic, intrinsic motivation, a motivation that doesn't have to be conjured or faked. Reinvest 75% of the money you're spending on motivational strategies. Reinvest it in strengths based selection, task alignment and repositioning. And when you make a hire that doesn't fit, spend a few dollars on strengths based outplacement.

Success Streaks

There is nothing like feeling like you're on a roll. *Strategic Coach* founder Dan Sullivan has a great momentum building strategy he calls, "3 Wins". He explains it here:

"Just before I go to bed, I review my day and decide what my three wins were. Regardless of anything else that happened during the day, I had three wins, and I visualize each of them in turn. The second part of the exercise is to imagine the day ahead and choose what my three biggest wins will be tomorrow. Doing this lets me fall asleep feeling good about the day I've just had and wake up excited about the day ahead. I go out and try to have the three wins I imagined, but I often have even bigger ones, which just gives me great material when I do the exercise again that night."

Dan has also created a great little app called *Win Streak* to record the "3 Wins" and it's free.

Another similar program is called *I Done This* and it has a free version as well. I have used this as my to-do list and can look back at any day to see what I accomplished. I can print out each and place them in a binder.

Strengths Strategist Marcus Buckingham asks, "What is your way as a leader of capturing and celebrating small wins?" Just like your to-do list, this is a terrific way to consistently monitor the delivery of your strengths. As you make your list, think about what strengths you can leverage in the activity. Consider writing the strength in front of the task.

CHAPTER 5

How I Manage Time

The following section of the book outlines time management concepts that are more personal. Most of the ideas I've presented are adaptations of strategies that I picked up from books, workshops, recordings, colleagues, family members, supervisors or those I've managed. I've tried and implemented every idea I'm presenting. Some were more appropriate for a particular project or season of work. These next ideas are personal favorites.

White Space

One of my coaches, Rich Fettke used to say, "We all need time to stop, be aware, resume control." We all need some white space in our lives. Pauses help make great music. It is the white space that helps make a great painting or photograph. Everything all jammed together creates darkness in your life. Stop reading for a moment and just breathe. Right now, take 3 deep breaths on 3 very slow counts of 3 for both the inhale and the exhale. Repeat this throughout the day. Do it every day.

Jim Fannin is one of the top coaches for elite athletes in the world. One of his core strategies is simply teaching his clients to stop regularly and breath deeply.

This is not a book about packing the most you can into every single day. Everyone needs structures in place that insure time off or breaks. If you're locked into a project that forces you to work from a non-talent, try to build in more breaks and time for restoration.

Work Flow

In their book, *Personal Kanban*, Jim Benson and Tonianne DeMaria Barry suggest that time management is something like freeway management. They write, "All too often we equate 'free time' with 'capacity'. We assume that if we don't have an activity scheduled, we can fit more work in. The calendar shows a free hour, so we must have time for another meeting or another phone call or another trip to the post office, right? *Wrong.*"

Benson and Barry suggest that research shows freeway congestion begins at somewhere around 65% capacity. As the freeway approaches 100% capacity, it ceases to be a freeway and becomes a parking lot.

We don't want activity gridlock. We want optimal activity throughput. The *Agile* system I introduce at the end of the book is designed to help us visualize our work and optimize the amount of work in progress. It's also a terrific tool that allows us to reflect on the strengths that will maximize productivity.

Oscillation

Tony Schwartz, founder of *The Energy Project* suggests human beings are built to work in productivity cycles with 90 minutes of work followed by 20 minutes of rest. Schwartz has often collaborated with *Human Performance Institute* founder Jim Loehr. They have similar findings and messages about the value of intervals and oscillation at work and in all kinds of athletic preparation and performance.

I have used different forms of oscillation or pulsing at work. My experience suggests that the 90/20 idea is valid but maybe a little too rigid. Sometimes you get on a roll and can blow right through the 90 minutes. Sometimes the demands make it necessary. It also depends on what the task is and how well you are suited to the task. In the section on Procrastination, I mentioned the 25 minute *Pomodoro Technique*. It includes oscillations with the (10+2)*5 suggested by Merlin Mann of *43folders*. Experiment with this and find your own version or versions of the 90/20 idea. In some cases, switching tasks or task types periodically can be useful. In general, try not to work from a non-talent for extended periods.

Full-Throttle Campaigns

Full-Throttle campaigns, based on the extra caffeinated drink, was an idea I came up with as a sales manager. This technique, similar to technology's "Crunching Strategy", was based on a method I found myself implementing naturally. It seemed to work fairly well universally if I built some flexibility into it.

While I'm by nature a marathoner, I found I needed to add harder kicks in occasionally to optimize my effectiveness.

When I was actually doing distance running, I incorporated Fartleks, which is a Swedish word meaning speed play. It's sometimes referred to as interval training. It offers huge gains in fitness and my run times started improving dramatically.

You can do the same thing with work. I did it when I was a contractor. I used it in sales and as a key structure as a sales manager. I found in sales settings, that a quarterly full-throttle campaign worked miracles. We routinely called on 40 to 50 accounts each week. But one week a quarter, we increased those calls to 100. For one week's time, that was a single focus.

As a sales manager, I gamified it with contests and prizes. I've used *Full-Throttle* campaigns as a job search coach with good results as well.

Most successful people use some version of a *Full-Throttle* campaign. Mark Twain wrote his top six books during two summers. These included *The Prince and the Pauper, Roughing It, Tom Sawyer, The Adventures of Huckleberry Finn, A Connecticut Yankee in King Arthur's Court* and *Life on the Mississippi.*

My goal is to write every single day. But my best productivity comes when I can work for a week or more at a time for at least 5 to 6 hours per day. Then Susy and I edit the writing in the afternoon.

Mozart reportedly preferred to write music for about one hour every morning immediately after getting up. But when he needed to, he would write night and day, foregoing sleep to finish a piece.

Navy Seals are trained to work around the clock for brief periods without sleep. Whatever you do, there's a *Full-Throttle* for you.

Day Types

Strategic Coach founder Dan Sullivan offers an entrepreneurial time management program that features Focus Days, Buffer Days and Preparation Days. He's based it on the time management strategies of elite entertainers.

My own system is slightly more nuanced with a few more categories.

Production Days are fully work focused based on my current optimal routine.

Project Days are work days oriented around a special outcome.

Preparation Days are work days focused on planning and getting ready for a main event such as a special presentation.

Play Days are days off and oriented around recreation or a fun activity such as a sporting event or concert.

Purposeful Puttering Days are for slow paced thinking, reading and often a trip to the bookstore.

Power Days are for complete restoration. They may include a church service and extra long naps.

In Between Time

My Grandpa Burns was a brilliant man with several patents to his name even though he only had a grammar school education. He got his start as a farm laborer. He went to his employer one day and asked if he could plant cotton between rows of the young walnut trees he was tending. He got the approval and that was his start as a farmer.

What can you plant in between rows? Where are the spaces in your life? Which spaces if properly utilized could be turned into profit for you and your family? Much of this book was written in the spaces of my life. Much of it was written one 3x5 card at a time in odd moments. This isn't unusual with authors. J.K. Rowling had the inspiration to write Harry Potter while waiting for a 4 hour train delay. Much of the early writing took place in what Rowling called "stolen moments at a café table".

An average game in professional sports lasts approximately 3 hours on television. If you know something about football, basketball and baseball, these games are full of timeouts with moments in-between quarters, halves and innings. In other words, actual play time is about 1/3 of total time.

That gives you 2 hours of time that you could spend on something profitable during a game. You could probably read several inspirational books during football season and never miss a play. You could outline or write a chapter for that book you've been meaning to write. You could write thank you notes to associates, volunteers, customers, employees, and anyone else who contributes to your life. You might memorize passages from the Bible.

You may be saying, "Dale, you're missing the point... football is my down time... I just want to relax and enjoy the game." Well then, you're missing my point. I'm just using football as an example. Everyone has spaces that can be packed with something profitable. And a nap is profitable. So is relaxation. I'm just asking you to consider all the spaces in your life and invest in some of them.

Make sure all or most of this space time is either invested in using your strengths or freeing up time that can be used on your strengths at another point.

The Waiting Kit

For many years I've kept a waiting kit with me. In some seasons it was a formalized pack of reading and writing material. I always have several books in my car. Usually my reading material is connected to what I'm currently writing about so that there is an interplay between reading and writing.

I have my waiting kit with me for every doctor's appointment. It has grown more digital over the years. I store books on my *iPad* and career oriented apps on my phone. I check email while standing in line. I keep a list of my signature strengths, my signature goals and writing outlines in *Trello*. I also review articles and other items in *Evernote*.

I've already shared my thoughts on "Windshield Time" in an earlier chapter. In a sense, I consider all drive time as waiting time. I listen to educational recordings constantly.

Red Zone

In football, the red zone is when the offense is anywhere inside your opponent's 20 yard line. You haven't crossed the goal line but you are within striking distance. Some football teams are great at driving the ball downfield but struggle when they get in the red zone. And football is about getting the ball across the goal line.

There is a correlation to this with any goal. I have several books that I've driven 80 yards downfield. But I haven't scored. They are not yet ready to publish. I'm still learning how to score in the red zone. One approach is to grind it out. That's what I'm doing right now.

Another approach, a more strengths based one, would be to hand the books over to a professional editor at the point it's in the red zone. Football teams do exactly this. They often bring in specialty players who are very adept at scoring in the red zone. It might be special blockers, a special full-back or a running back.

Baseball has done this with pitching in recent decades. Professional teams have starting pitchers, middle relievers, set-up pitchers and closers who only pitch in the last inning.

Phase Type

Bobb Biehl has an assessment that is designed to help identify the phase of a project where you shine. He uses building terminology. Are you an Architect type who thrives on design? Are you a Builder who organizes and makes a project run on time? Are you a Craftsman who loves to make things? Or are you a Detailer, a punch-list person, who finishes up the project?

Marketing expert Seth Godin refers to these phase types as stances: "The Scientist does experiments. Sometimes they work, sometimes they fail. She takes good notes. Comes up with a theory. Works to disprove it. Publishes the work. Moves on to more experiments.

The Engineer builds things that work. Take existing practices, weave them together and create a bridge that won't fall down, write code that won't crash, design an HR department that's efficient and effective.

The Operations Manager takes the handbook and executes on it. Brilliantly. Promises, kept. Hands on, full communications, on time.

The scientist invents the train. The engineer builds it out. The operations manager makes it run on time.

Operations managers shouldn't do experiments. Scientists shouldn't ask for instructions on what to do next. Engineers shouldn't make stuff up..."

These are all innate strengths and it's good to know which part of a project you thrive on.

Your Zone

Ted Williams, by many estimations, was the best hitter in baseball history. He was certainly the best hitter of his era. He was the last player to hit over .400 and he did it while hitting for power.

He began to share his theories in a book titled, *The Science of Hitting*, in the late 1960's. Williams observed that his strike zone was 77 balls in size, 7 balls wide and 11 balls high. Williams worked hard on self awareness with regard to his strengths and weaknesses as a hitter. He was aware that his batting average was the worst, only .230 on the ball farthest low and outside. He knew with certainty what his batting average was in every one of those 77 ball placements. And he focused only on swinging at those pitches that were in his high average zone.

Every baseball hitter has a unique zone of high performance. Among the best hitters, these zones are very different. Williams' strength was as a dead pull hitter who only hit toward right field. Opposing defenses implemented the famed, and unprecedented, "Williams Shift", setting up more players on the right side of second base. Williams didn't adjust. He stayed in his "wheelhouse" doing what he did best. What's your wheelhouse?

Strong Sleep

I have never had any trouble falling asleep but since my mid-twenties I've struggled with the 2nd half of the sleep cycle. Recently I've found Magnesium Lactate from *Standard Process* to be a huge help. I've tried many other magnesium products and none of them worked at all. Apparently not all magnesium is equally bioavailable. I've also found that using Sucralose (sometimes sold as *Splenda)* at any point during the day will negatively impact my 2nd sleep cycle. Initially I thought it might be a mid-afternoon green tea. But with repeated experiments, I isolated the sweetener. I've also found that a certain brand of turmeric agitates me and a particular veggie burger inhibits my 2nd sleep cycle. I suspect this is all very individual. If sleep is a problem for you, turn your bedroom into a sleep lab. Your *Fitbit* will even record your sleep patterns. Currently, I'm sleeping better than ever!

My wife loves white noise and we take the machine everywhere.

Different high performing individuals have wide variations on how much sleep they require for optimal functioning. Buckminster Fuller was a scientific genius who reported sleeping only 2 hours per night. Albert Einstein reported sleeping 10 hours a night. Music star Mariah Carey reportedly sleeps 15 hours surrounded by 20 humidifiers.

Identify your unique sleep path. This may take a lot of experimenting and some study to discover what has worked for others. What works for them might work for you. A huge dividend will come to those who discover their own special blend of sleep.

Strong Naps

Some people call these power naps, but I call them strong naps. The power nap is generally 20 minutes long. The strong nap is based on your unique physiological make-up and needs on any given day. This includes not taking a nap. My wife hates naps and she doesn't need them. I've worked hard to train her, spent hours trying to get her to lie down just for a few minutes, believing that if she could just experience one great nap she'd be hooked. It's not her deal.

I come from a long line of nappers on both sides of the family. My dad worked 18 hour days year-in-year-out while I was growing up. And he can also sleep anywhere anytime. He's napped at *World Series* baseball games, through the talks of the best motivational speakers on the planet, and on most Sundays at church. Both of my grandfathers were nappers. One on doctor's orders.

NASA research done in the 1990's, shows that a 26 minute nap improved cognitive performance by 34% and alertness by 54%. Dozens of top companies encourage napping and in many cases, provide napping pods or other spaces to optimize the habit. These companies include *Ben & Jerry's* (naps and ice cream too!), *Google, Cisco, Zappos, Uber, Proctor & Gamble* and *PriceWaterhouseCoopers*.

Experiment. You may find it a huge performance boost!

Winston Churchill believed his naps doubled his productivity
Eleanor Roosevelt napped
Oil tycoon John Rockefeller napped in his office every day
Leonardo da Vinci took 15 minute naps every four hours
Napoleon napped daily
Margaret Thatcher napped between 2:30 and 3:30 daily
Thomas Edison was a big napper who kept a bed at his lab
Ronald Reagan napped in cabinet meetings
Bill Clinton says he can sleep standing up
President Kennedy lunched in bed and napped for 1-2 hours
Lyndon Johnson took his daily naps at 3:30

The current science on napping suggests:

- Nap between 1pm and 4pm
- Do it somewhere quiet
- Nap for 20 minutes
- If you exceed 20 minutes, go for 90 minutes

Experiment and see what works for you. I have always napped, almost everyday. The only exception was a two-year period between 2013 to 2015. I think it hurt my productivity. I still take longer naps on Saturday and Sunday, often for 90 minutes.

Some believe naps will be the new coffee. Great idea!

Good "Carma"

Like my desk, my car can get very cluttered. When I was working out of my car every day, it was an even bigger struggle. This is not a book about space organization, keeping a clean desk or car. Yet, disorganization can become a time use issue. My friend Brad Vander Ley was out riding with one of his reps one day and decided to use a stop watch to count the time that rep spent in his trunk pulling together sell sheets for leave behind packets. The rep spent approximately 1.5 hours in his trunk that day.

Most jobs have mundane tasks that can be done without a lot of thought. This is true for teachers, salespeople, managers and anyone who does knowledge work or participates in today's creative economy. Put your materials together at home or a special work space so that you don't have to pull them together on the fly. There are also any number of ways to maximize your time when pulling teaching, selling or training packets together. Here are 3 ideas:

1. Keep your information sheets in files and containers that make it easy to quickly pull packets together. Put a stop watch on yourself so that you know approximately how long it takes per packet.

2. Put your packets together during a favorite TV Show, while watching a movie, or while viewing a sporting event. You could do it during commercials. My wife is a great time manager and she chops veggies while watching TV. If teaching, managing or sales isn't your work, some of your tasks can be done this way.

3. Outsource it to your kids. This will save you time, teach them the value of work and earning money, and involve them as a valued team member. You might also involve a spouse but make sure they are willing. I wouldn't expect it especially if they have their own job or career including homemaking and child rearing.

If you work from your car, make it a regular practice to reorganize and clean. This may be daily, weekly or monthly depending on your situation. If you transport clients like realtors often do, you may want to spend some time cleaning each day. If your work involves a lot of travel as mine did, weekly or monthly may be your best bet. If you can afford it, take it to a good car wash and include a nice scent.

Simplify

One of my favorite cartoons pictures an elderly man tired of being slowed down at airport security, walking through the machine in a speedo. I'm not voting for clip-on ties in this segment but there are some ways of dressing and some items of clothing that save time. Wrinkle free clothing saves ironing time. Shirt stays may save you awkward moments and the constant shirt re-tucking. Salespeople and plumbers alike could benefit from that anti-wardrobe malfunction advice. Loafers save time tying your shoes not just once but many times throughout the day. It's apparently hard to find shoe strings that want to stay tied. Zig Ziglar traveled every week and was always ending up in destinations without his belt. So he switched to a pant style that didn't require one.

Albert Einstein wore khaki pants so he wouldn't have to think about what to wear. He didn't wear socks either. When shown a can of shaving cream he said, "That's too many soaps". He was very concerned about simplifying the mundane details of his life so he could focus on what was really important to him.

Many very successful people wear the same thing every day. They manage their time, simplify their life and reduce decisions so they can focus on the issues that matter most.

Steve Jobs ordered his famous black mock turtleneck shirts in huge quantities and completed his daily outfit with jeans and new balance sneakers.

Grateful Dead guitarist Jerry Garcia dressed similarly with a black t-shirt and jeans.

Facebook founder Mark Zuckerberg wears a grey t-shirt and black hoodie.

Author Fran Lebowitz wears a black pant suit with a white blouse.

Barak Obama now wears only grey or blue suits.

R&B singer Janelle Monae wears only black and white.

Inventor Dean Kamen wears denim shirts and denim pants.

Jean Nouvel is a famed French architect who wears all white in the summer and all black in the winter.

Henry David Thoreau wrote, "Our life is frittered away by detail. Simply, simplify." I can tell you from experience that decision fatigue is a real psychological condition. You can easily become mentally exhausted from making so many mundane unimportant decisions.

Personally, I've tried to limit my wardrobe choices and I've tried to do the same thing with my food selection. When traveling, I focused on staying at one hotel chain, *Hampton Inns*. They are comfortable and consistent. I always knew where everything was and I racked up thank you points. As a bonus, they are a company that has wholeheartedly embraced the strengths movement!

Systems

The universe is constructed around 589 known multi-planetary systems. Our ecological system is comprised of an estimated 8.7 million species. There are 11 major systems in the human body.

You have to develop systems. Real Estate giant Ralph Roberts wrote, "Systems can set you free... A system can be as simple as using blue file folders for buyers and red file folders for sellers. A system is nothing more than a way to help you keep track of your business. Your systems can include checklists, form letters, schedules and worksheets. As your business grows in complexity so will your systems... All the systems in my office range from simple ones to fairly complex ones. The important thing for you to do is to start creating your own."

Most of America's great businesses are founded on equally great systems. J. Willard Marriott set up 66 steps for cleaning a hotel room in less than a half-hour. *UPS* drivers are taught 340 precise methods of how to correctly deliver a package. Ray Kroc was enamored with the systems he found at the *McDonald Brothers Hamburger* restaurant in San Bernardino. He built on those to build an enormous franchise system. The essence of a franchise really is the system.

But systems aren't just for business. Artists use systems to consistently produce a flow of work. Charles Schulz identified twelve devices that he repeatedly used to write his successful comic strip. They included, *The Kite-eating tree, Schroeder's music, Linus's blanket, Lucy's psychiatry booth, Snoopy's doghouse, Snoopy himself, Woodstock, The Red Baron, The football episodes, The baseball games, The Great Pumpkin, The little red-haired girl.*

As Ralph Roberts said, "The important thing is for you to start creating your own." Or you can build on someone else's system. You don't have to reinvent the wheel. But you do need to customize it. E. Stanley Jones was one of my favorite writers when I was in my early twenties. Jones wrote, "Very often we create a system which only we can run, for it reflects our genius, and then call other people inefficient who cannot run it because it does not express their genius." This is such a great cautionary thought.

Consider this concept when you adopt other people's systems. But also consider it when you're hiring and plugging new people into an existing program. You can't expect an employer to change their entire way of doing things to accommodate your unique strength set. When considering a position, try to identify the existing systems and think about how well you will fit. And when hiring, make sure the top candidate will fit the established way you do business. Whenever you can, give your employees an opportunity to create their own systems or adapt yours to fit them better.

Time Tools

Not long ago, time management was a very tool focused endeavor. *Day-Timers*, *Day-Runners*, *Franklin Planners*, *Covey Planners*, *At-A-Glance* and *Filofax* were some of the great choices on the market. I used to love going to the *Franklin Planner* stores and then the *Franklin-Covey* stores that were popping up in malls around the country.

As digital options began to flood the market, the number of choices has exploded. Your hand-held smart device has dozens of solid options for free or a very few dollars.

You may still need some configuration of a calendar, a to-do list and a contact manager. The contact manager is probably a part of your smart device. I recommend either the *iCalendar* by *Apple* or the *Google Calendar.* If you're in sales,

Salesforce.com has an end-to-end solution. That leaves you with a million choices for a to-do list. Don't overlook the 3x5 card, a *Moleskine* notebook or a simple letter size pad. They are retro, but they work. Digitally I'm fond of *I Done This.* I've also moved many of my planning lists over to *Trello* because it fits so nicely with the *Agile* platform that I will share toward the end of this book. And *Evernote* is a growing part of my arsenal.

Rule #3

Seattle Seahawks football coach Pete Carroll has only 3 rules for the team. Rule #3 is always be early. Carroll says he wants his players in the meeting before they start with their playbooks open and ready to learn. He makes the connection between organization, planning and execution on the field with organization, planning and execution off the field. Carroll also teaches that being early is respectful to teammates and coaches.

Being late is not a weakness. It's a character issue. It's failure to keep your word. Lateness erodes trust.

In her terrific book, *Pathways to Possibility*, Rosamund Stone Zander reflects on Carroll's Rule Number 3. She writes, "Be Early. What powerful little words! What an amazing third rule! The player who lives by 'be early' puts himself in charge of his life. It is virtually impossible to be on time, even though people will persistently aim for it, because the time allotted to 'on time' is only a split second, whereas being early and being late have eons to play with. If you aim for being on time you will miss and veer to one or the other and be out of control no matter which side you land on, because you won't be where you intended to be. If you decide to be early, you are always in charge; you will show up as a considerate person as well as a paragon of responsibility."

Atmospheres

I love snow globes, the kind you can shake up and create snow. It's a reminder that we're all designed to be environment positive creators. In fact, we create environments constantly whether we are aware of it or not. Singer Jimmy Buffett says, "You can take the weather with you." When you walk in a room, a lot more shows up than you might imagine. In fact, some would suggest we even bring a spiritual entourage. On my best days, I've been told I bring peace into a room, sometimes creativity and wisdom. On my worst days, I bring some things I'm not proud of, including a spirit of criticism and fatigue.

I'm learning how to check the environment at the door. I'm learning how to do a quick check up on what I'm bringing in the door with me.

Good time management is often the result of setting up the right environment. It's about controlling atmospheres. It might be inspirational paint colors, pictures or just the right music. It includes recruiting the right people for the team.

Staging the Job

I come from a construction background growing up in a family business. One of the things my father taught me very early was the importance of staging the job properly. It meant getting all the needed materials and equipment on the worksite ahead of time, either for the day or an entire project. Mid-day trips to the lumber yard or back to the shop for equipment were huge time wasters. My dad believed that the stager was the most important role on the team.

The stagers often had a role during the flow of work, seeing to it that equipment and materials were in place. They were like point guards on a basketball team who specialize in setting up other players to score. *Phoenix Suns* guard Steve Nash was the best I ever saw at this. I never watched Steve Nash play to see him score baskets. I watched him play to see these dazzling assists, helping his teammates score baskets.

In great businesses, managers play this role. They specialize in setting other people up to score. Great managers know the strengths and weaknesses of their people and get them work that matches their genius.

Think about your next project. Are all the materials in place? Are all the needed tools in place? Are the right people in the right roles? Do you know what each worker's genius is? That's great time management!

Off The Field Time Management

I always talk about "<u>On</u> The Field" time management which is what you do during the time you are working. But I also think it's important to be aware of "<u>Off</u> The Field" time management as well. How you spend your time when you are not working is no one's business... but it should be your business and it could have tremendous impact on your success and earnings.

Let me share a personal story. At around age 40, I got the bug to play baseball again... not softball but real baseball. I joined a team in a league that played on Saturday or Sunday and had the time of my life. I found that I still had pretty good arm strength and was asked to become a pitcher. For two summers I was out there on the diamond. We won league championships and I made the all-star team both years. Does it get any better than that?

Only one problem... after pitching on Sunday, it was Wednesday before I could crawl out of bed due to the soreness in my body. I would have no energy until the middle end of the week at which point I would begin to think about the upcoming game again. My job took a back seat and my income suffered. Honestly, I could have lost my job.

After 2 years, I reluctantly retired and never looked back. My income went up and within a couple more years I was promoted into management. Maybe baseball isn't your deal, but I'm willing to bet you have a deal... something you love that could get in the way of using your real strengths to make real contributions that will eventually payoff for you and your family. I'm not suggesting you can't have hobbies. In fact you need them to live a well balanced life. But a hobby should enhance your career, not detract from it.

Another potential pitfall is volunteer work and church work. This one is so easy to justify because you are helping people. I have volunteered many hours in my church so I'm not suggesting that you can't or shouldn't do this. Just do it with a firm grasp on the fact that your family and often others in your company are depending on your productivity to insure they have enough to live on. Being a great volunteer while failing or even putting out mediocre effort at work isn't acceptable. And it doesn't honor God.

The Time Fast

Most of us are familiar with a food fast. This is where we go a short period of time without eating any food, solid food (liquid only such as water or juice), or a particular type of food such as bread or bad carbohydrates. Let me suggest that a powerful time management strategy is the "time fast".

Simply put, a time fast is foregoing an activity (usually a pleasant one) for a short period of time in order to put full focus on time critical results. It may mean something as simple as no video games, internet, newspapers or television for a week or two. It may mean missing a week of softball. It may even mean minimizing for a very short time something that is a higher priority. For example, you may have to sit down with your family and say, "Mom or dad is in the middle of finishing a big project this week and I won't have the time I usually do for you. But next week things will be back to normal." Of course you have to watch and make sure that you keep your commitments. Next week your time fast may mean foregoing some work time.

Most of us tend to think of fasting as foregoing something pleasant or pleasurable. From a work or productivity perspective, you might try the opposite for a day or two. Set up a couple of days where you only do work that maximizes your natural talent and passion. Set up a daily time frame where you only work in an area of strength. I know this sounds like disciplining yourself to eat ice cream, but try it.

Shorten Your Season

The football season starts in August, if you count pre-season games, and culminates sometime in early February with the Super Bowl. In recent history we have had a 16 game regular season with one bye week for each team. Then playoffs began in January. I love to watch football on television and occasionally attend a college or professional game when it fits with the rest of what I have going on. But a few years ago, I decided it wasn't a great investment of time to spend 8 hours on Sunday watching football for 16 weeks or more. That's about 128 hours a year that just wasn't a high payoff.

So I shortened "my" football season. I chopped off most of the regular season with the exception of a few big games. I really dial it in starting in January. You can apply the principle to any sport or any activity. Cut down your knitting season. Maybe it's baseball season for you. Maybe it's hockey. I once heard leadership guru John Maxwell comment that a basketball game is really "played" in the last 5 minutes... the rest of the game is really just warm up and each team feeling each other out. I know people who play 36 holes of golf. That's all day.

The principle also applies to work activities. Maybe you're spending 80-90 hours a week at work. Are you really getting a big payoff for the extra 20 or 30 hours? I know of a pastor with a church of over 30,000 in attendance each week. When he started the church, he made a commitment to God and his family that he would build the biggest church he could, working no more than 45 hours a week.

I'm not suggesting that you take away anything that really contributes to your life. I'm just asking that you really consider what <u>does</u> contribute to your life and make choices accordingly.

Boundaries

One of the great things about outside selling is that you make your own schedule. One of the awful things about outside selling is that you make your own schedule.

It's either great or awful and you get to choose. You can work it out so that you attend most of your son's band performances and your daughter's karate tournaments and still get your work done. You can also work it so that your family is constantly interfering in your business workday to the extent that both you and they suffer.

You have to establish some boundaries around your business and enforce those boundaries with a kind firmness. Your spouse or kids may not understand. They may think that because you control your own schedule that you can drop everything every time someone needs a ½-gallon of milk.

People in job search mode struggle with this greatly. If you are out of work, you just went into outside sales and the product is you.

Learn to manage your boundaries quickly or you will quickly find yourself struggling or ultimately failing.

One big boundary issue in the age of cell phones is taking personal calls and texts on business time. Again, the great thing about this job is that you can usually be available in a true emergency. But true emergencies don't happen every day or even every week. You may have to educate your family and renegotiate your relationships. I have ridden with marketing reps that get call after call from their spouse and/or kids. This doesn't work.

In the age of smart phones, texting and personal email have both become productivity issues. One of my favorite photographs is of John Kennedy in the Oval Office. His young son is playing under the desk. Part of love is giving those close to you accessibility. Loved ones need to be able to reach you 24/7. But those loved ones must also respect your work.

The reverse is equally true. You've got to have family time that remains work free. Always being accessible to the office is just as big a problem.

Get in the habit of being where you are.

Saying No

Stephen Covey said, "You can say 'no' and smile only when there is a bigger 'yes' burning inside you." The first step in strengths based time management is finding that thing that burns inside you. I call that passion. Strengths based time management is all about saying "No" to most of the activities outside of your strengths, especially your passion and talents. It is about saying "No" to activities that don't lead to your signature destinations. And it's about saying "No" to routes or methods that don't line up with your signature strategy.

Of course there will always be exceptions. I was just interrupted from this writing to fix a broken bed frame. Anything mechanical is clearly outside of both my passion and talent. Sometimes you just have to get it done.

If you are a new employee at any age, I don't recommend playing the strengths card anytime in the first three months and maybe the first year. The exception would be if you are fortunate enough to have gone to work for a strengths based company.

Changing Plays

Michael Jordan said that he would decide what to do with the basketball after he left the ground and was soaring through the air. All of the best football quarterbacks read the defense and change or alter play calls at the line of scrimmage.

Good time management often means having a good plan "B", a good plan "C" and sometimes a good plan "Z". Too often we only bring one option to the table. We have to be able to move quickly off the original plan.

One way to accomplish this is through Scenario Planning. This idea was made famous by a group of strategists who worked at *Royal Dutch Shell* in the 1970's. They decided to prepare strategic plans for multiple possible futures as they related to the oil industry. This was in contrast to the preferred future that other oil companies were planning for. When an oil crisis hit, they were the only company that was prepared. They easily shifted their plan and made billions as a result.

Timing

I have already talked about Prime Time and how it may be different in each industry and for every account, vendor or partner you work with. I've also covered Personal Prime Time, which is about when you personally are the most alert and effective.

Mark Di Vincenzo's book, *Buy Ketchup In May And Fly At Noon* introduces this very well. It offers a lot of ideas like:

Best time of day to do the most difficult task – Between 10am and 11am due to cortisol, blood sugar and alertness. This challenges the classic frog eating theory.

From a strengths perspective, the answer would be based on your circadian rhythm.

Best time of day to have your picture taken – Late morning or early afternoon. It gives you more time to shake off morning eye puffiness and catches you before fatigue sets in.

Best time to make a presentation – Mid morning. You and your audience are most alert and your voice is rested.

Best time to reach 24/7 tech support – 6am to 8am regardless of your time zone. Note: *Apple's* staff is always rated the highest. Buy a *Mac*. It will save you time 10 ways.

These tips may sound superfluous but there really is a best time to do almost anything.

Times

"The sons of Issachar understood the times and knew what Israel should do..." This passage from I Chronicles 12:32 in the Jewish-Christian Scriptures has fascinated me for many years. Some people have a knack for recognizing the seasons of life. Each season of life has a strength or potential strength that comes with it. This is true for individuals, business units, entire organizations and nations.

To get in sync with the times and your unique season of life, is certainly an often overlooked secret of success. If you don't have this knack, try to cultivate a relationship with someone who does. This person will be a special kind of strengths-spotter. Ideally they will understand your unique strengths and help you match them up to your season of life.

Pace

"Success comes to those who run their own race, at their own pace, on their own track."
~Tom Volkar

Tortoises and hares can both be winners... but only if they learn to be their best selves. I tend to be a steady plodding tortoise. I can muster up a hare's speed for up to a week and maybe two weeks at a time. Beyond that, it doesn't work for me. A guaranteed path to failure is to impose a time temperament on yourself that doesn't fit who you are. Another path to failure, is to impose your time temperament on someone else.

I'm purely talking about your overall day-in day-out flow of activity. If you are a sprinter then sprint. If you are a marathoner then work in harmony with who God made you. There are gold medalists in both types of events. This concept is contrasted with giving 100% - 100% of the time. The world's fastest man can't maintain sub 10-second 100-meter dash speeds while running a 440. Usain Bolt is currently the world's fastest man... in the 100-meter dash. He has never even run a full mile. He focuses on the races he can win.

All high achievers pace themselves. When Tiger Woods was playing the best golf of his career, he didn't play every tournament. In the course of a year, he took several weeks off. He focused on four major tournaments that included the *Masters*, the *U.S. Open*, the *British Open* and the *PGA Championship*.

Dr. Bob Rotella is one of America's top sports psychologists and has worked with many elite athletes, rock stars and business leaders. Bob says, "If you think trying your hardest is what doing your best is all about, you're confused. You must make a decision to throw away any attitudes that sound good and look good but don't work."

Former *Navy Seal* instructor, Richard "Mack" Machowicz agrees. In his book *Unleash The Warrior Within* he writes, "You often hear the expression 'giving it your all' or 'giving 110 percent effort.' I don't believe in thinking that way, or training that way. You can't put 110 percent into anything because it's against the laws of physics. You only have 100 percent, and I believe that the closer you push yourself to 100 percent, the closer you are to shutting your body down. You can run your car at top speed for a few seconds, but after that it starts to shake, and ultimately falls apart. The more effective way to think is to aim for bringing all your skills to 80 percent of your maximum, in whatever you do. At this point you are able to think, to use your body to stay in balance and harmony, to flow rather than force. In sports performance, researchers call this the 'steady state', because your body systems are running at an efficient level."

I agree with "Mack" on this completely and I would only add that 80% looks different for different people. Sometimes I take an electronic metronome into my Time Management Classes. I turn the speed up and down between:

Tic...Tic...Tic and **Tic.............Tic..............Tic.**

Not only is everyone different in what they can productively maintain, they are unique in each season of life.

Time Shifting - Task Synchronization

Many tasks have an optimal rhythm built into them. When I hung wallpaper, I had to set my pace to the unique qualities of the material. Vinyl worked quickly. Paper was a little slower. Foils were extremely slow.

Sometimes that rhythm is a combination of your time temperament and how it fits together with the task itself. In the case of a sales call or classroom presentation, it may be syncing up your temperament with the temperament of others. You may also need to sync up with the type of information.

Every presentation has an optimal pace, time frame (duration), time of day and arrangement of content that is unique or different from any other. Discovering these factors and aligning with them may get you a lot of business.

Other more mundane tasks like putting together information packets also have an optimal rhythm. You could get faster, but faster isn't always better.

CHAPTER 6

Shifting to Strengths

In this chapter, I want to introduce you to four strategies that will help you shift your time toward your strengths.

The first strategy is to simply become aware that successful people operate very differently. As an example, we'll look at two specific roles, the Supreme Court Justice and a Military General.

The second strategy is a way to make your days progressively more strengths oriented. I call it *STRENGTHSPATH* Math.

The third strategy is retiring your weaknesses.

Lastly, I will summarize with a grouping of seven options to consider when you find yourself in work that doesn't fit.

We have nine Supreme Court Justices. Each Justice does the same job, although the Chief Justice may have some oversight responsibilities. Political leanings, philosophy, values and beliefs aside, they all approach their jobs quite differently. There is a wide range of style, personality and temperament among the nine justices.

Anthony Kennedy leans forward to ask questions. Often these questions display feelings and take an emotional tone. But rarely do these expressions give away how he will actually vote.

Justice **Samuel Alito** also asks questions. They often cut straight to the heart of the issue the court is hearing. But unlike Kennedy, his questions often give away his thoughts, feelings and how he will likely vote.

Stephen Breyer is known for his complex hypothetical questions. Some have ranked him as the most talkative Justice.

Justice **Clarence Thomas** is the least talkative and rarely asks a question. He went over 6 years without making a single inquiry. In a 2009 *C-Span* interview Thomas said, "I think there are far too many questions. Some members of the court like that interaction. I prefer to listen and think it through more quietly."

The three women Justices, **Ruth Bader Ginsburg, Sonia Sotomayor** and **Elena Kagan** are completely different. They often jockey to be the first to ask a question. They sometimes interrupt a lawyer's initial presentation in the first few syllables. And often these questions are sharply worded. Ginsburg's questions come out slowly and clearly enunciated. Kagan tends to ask big picture analytical questions. Sotomayor can be demanding of lawyers and is not afraid to butt heads with other Justices.

Anthony Scalia (recently deceased) was the funniest and most likely to bring laughter into the courtroom. Next to Breyer, Scalia was ranked as the second most talkative.

As the Chief Justice, **John Roberts** reins in the lawyers and, at times, his fellow Justices. He usually saves his questions for last.

What about World War II generals like **Eisenhower, Bradley, Patton** and **MacArthur**? Surely they were similar in talent and temperament. Not so.

Eisenhower was a talented administrator. He was a people person and a gifted diplomat. Temperamentally he was well-suited to keep all the allied generals fighting Germans and not each other. But he didn't have the battlefield talent of the other three. Eisenhower could also match Patton word for word with ferocious outbursts when the circumstances called for it.

MacArthur was a gifted administrator like Eisenhower but more of an egomaniac. His staff loved him but he was often in conflict with his peers.

Patton was a loose canon whose real genius was on the battlefield. He tended to not think before he spoke and, unlike Eisenhower, had no sense of the need to build coalitions with allies.

Bradley was a great team player who was an excellent planner and meticulous in his execution. The foundation of Bradley's success was a strong ability to grasp all the pieces on a huge moving battlefield.

The point of these examples is that there are a lot of ways to be successful at the same job. According to family therapist Virginia Satir, there are at least 250 ways to wash the dishes. In my work as a manager, I have observed sales people reach the pinnacle of success with quite different strengths and ways of going about their day to day work. This is possible with most jobs, including the job of running the country. In my book, *The STRENGTHSPATH PRINCIPLE*, I cover a few of the U.S. Presidents in some detail.

Do *STRENGTHSPATH* Math

Try the mathematical approach to change. Every week identify one work activity that you either hate or aren't very good at. **SUBTRACT** that activity. Stop doing it. If the activity is essential, trade with someone. Hire someone. Find an intern. Outsource it. Then **ADD** one activity you love every week. Figure out what you love doing and then figure out how to integrate it with your current duties.

Stay with this adding and subtracting method until you've created your dream job.

A few readers should start looking for a new job immediately. Your job fits so poorly it's a mental health issue. I recently talked to a very gifted woman who had awards all over her wall for achievements at work. But she went home and cried herself to sleep every night. She quit and loves what she does now.

There are two kinds of total career makeovers, internal and external. With internal makeovers you make an effort to stay in the same company. With external makeovers you change companies.

Progressively Retire Your Non-Talents

Dr. Robert Schuller, founder of the *Crystal Cathedral Congregation* in Garden Grove, California, is a hero of mine at so many levels. My Mom, Dad, both sets of Grandparents and myself tuned into his weekly *Hour of Power* broadcasts. I still have my Dad's copy of Dr. Schuller's early book, *Move Ahead With Possibility Thinking*. His teaching and ministry got me through some of the most difficult times of my life. In one of Schuller's later books, *If It Is To Be, It's Up To Me,* he writes on the concept of progressive early retirement. Schuller begins:

"How do I find the time to manage a weekly world-wide television ministry? And write books? And build a strong and happy family based on a loving marriage that's close to a joyous fiftieth anniversary?

I learned early in life how and when to 'retire'. I've now passed the forty-year anniversary in my ministerial work. At the end of my first year on the job as pastor I began to 'retire'. I retired from the job of janitor, for example. I haven't cleaned floors or toilets since! And that retirement freed up time for other duties. At the end of my second year I retired from my job as secretary, no longer typing my own letters. I found time to do other worthwhile church work. At the end of my third year, I retired as business manager. I haven't deposited money or written a check for the parish since then. I was released to use my time more productively. At the end of my fourth year, I retired as a department leader and teacher. I found the church a better replacement, and I had more time to write. At the end of my fifth year, then sixth year – yes, every passing year – I retired from further time consuming duties. At the end of my tenth year I finally retired as marriage counselor. The counseling center was opened and staffed as part of our ministry, and I found a lot of time – time that was instantly filled with new ideas that needed top priority on my clock and calendar. At the end of my fifteenth year we launched the television ministry, and I retired as the senior minister managing the staff of a large local congregation. At the end of my twenty-fifth year I retired as my car driver. I can now read books, dictate letters, and read my mail – all from the back seat of a car. At the end of my fortieth year I retired from five days a week in the office to become a minister at large in the world, filling a role only my face and name could fill."

Schuller continues, " Learn how to retire selectively from those duties you've always done. Focus on the role where you're irreplaceable. You'll be surprised at how well, wisely and fruitfully your time will then be managed." He exhorts us later in the book with some advice on what might inform our retirement choices when he says, "Look for something you enjoy and are pretty good at, and go for it."

When should you start this early retirement program? I think age 8 works. The school system will object and you will still need to pitch in with family chores, but why not start early? Tiger Woods did and so did Warren Buffett.

Finding Yourself in Work You Don't Enjoy

All of us will have some frog swallowing to do in life and at work. But if you find yourself swallowing frogs all day long, you need to make change. My advice: Don't quit your current job before you've received a written job offer that fits better. There are some exceptions but they are rare. But eventually…

"If it doesn't fit you have to quit."
~Unknown wise person

The late *Tonight Show* host, Johnny Carson advised, "Never continue in a job you don't enjoy. If you are happy in what you are doing, you will like yourself, you will have inner peace and if you have that, along with physical health, you will have more success than you could possibly have imagined." John Maxwell said, "You will never fulfill your destiny doing work you despise."

7 Ways to Change Jobs

There are at least seven ways to change jobs. You can experiment with four of the ways while staying in your current position. The fifth way may allow you to stay with the same company in a different role. Ideas six and seven are more dramatic moves, although each can often be accomplished in ways that reduce risk:

1. **Restructure Your Job** – Change the who, when, where, aspects of your work
2. **Reduce Your Job Tasks** – Specialize or reduce variety
3. **Expand Your Job Tasks** – Generalize or increase variety
4. **Change How You Do It** - Adjust your approach
5. **Change Jobs** – Task Sets – If you're in sales go into accounting
6. **Change Companies** – Align with an organization that matches your values
7. **Start a Business** – Take on some side work

I recommend *The 10% Entrepreneur* by Patrick McGinnis and *The Leap* by Rick Smith. They outline low-risk ways of getting started.

Many people are doing what they are designed to do, but only partially. Maybe you are in a situation where half of what you do fits very well but the other half doesn't. There isn't always a solution to this. But sometimes you can negotiate a restructuring of your position with your company. Sometimes you can get it accomplished "off the books" by trading activities.

Some workers would be much more effective if they were doing a very focused subset of their current responsibilities. They need to specialize. An individualized version of what Jack Welch did with *General Electric* would be perfect.

When Welch took over *G.E.* in 1981, it was a respectable company. But it was a very diverse company that included 350 different businesses. Welch believed *G.E.* could be even better. What was his strategy? He used the *STRENGTHSPATH Principle*. He Discovered what *G.E.* was best at, Developed those businesses, and then Delivered them in a very focused way out in the marketplace. In his own words, Welch describes the process:

"To the hundreds of businesses and product lines that made up the company we applied a single criterion: can they be number 1 or number 2 at whatever they do in the world marketplace? Of the 348 businesses or product lines that could not, we closed some and divested others. Their sale brought in almost $10 billion. We invested $18 billion in the ones that remained and further strengthened them with 17 billion worth of acquisitions. What remained in 1989 were 14 world-class businesses, each one either first or second in the world market in which it participates."

Most workers could benefit from a personalized version of what *G.E.* did. Think about how you can close down some of the activities you aren't the best at. Sell off or outsource some others.

A few workers would be much more effective if they did just the opposite and expanded their duties. Some people are very gifted with broad categories of work and thrive on variety. They need to generalize.

CHAPTER 7

Time Management Jazz

In this section, I want to draw a comparison between music, specifically jazz, and how you can maximize your time. Jazz is unique for it's improvisation, call and response communication, complex rhythms, optimal venue and its ability to incorporate nearly anything that happens. Each of these components can be symbolically related to time management. For those of you that love metaphor or even a poetic approach to time management, this might be helpful.

Improvisation

Jazz is a unique form of music because improvisation is a key component. Just as you won't experience two identical days, you will never hear the same jazz piece performed the same way twice. It would be recognizable as the same song but would be altered. Jazz is about feeling the audience, seeing how they respond, and adjusting your set and style. **Great time management should be improvisational as well.** It should fit the circumstances and the people involved, incorporating on-the-fly adjustments in the moment.

Old models of time management training were much more rigid. You were handed the score and expected to play it precisely. Today, time management is much more like jazz. I may follow a set flow and structure, but with plenty of room for improvisation depending on what is happening on each unique day.

With jazz you have to know and be able to perform the score with spot-on accuracy. Each note and phrase must be in place. And then you make it your own. This is true with strengths based time management. You've got to have your structure, sequence, phrases... what you do and when you do it, down cold. Don't walk into your daily gig and just play random notes and phrases. You've got to have a very clear idea of what you want to have happen, of what impact you want to make at work.

The greatest improvisational performer of all-time is well-known to the public for everything except his improvisation. Even when sitting in with other musicians he couldn't resist changing their compositions on the fly. The improviser was Johann Sebastian Bach. **In the 18th century, improvisation was regarded as an integral component of serious music**. Bach and other composers of the time rarely spelled out parts for each instrument. They were expected to riff. When notes were specified on the sheet, musicians routinely threw in improvised flourishes. Like my wife Susy, who when cooking, sprinkles an extra dash of this and sprig of that.

Bach was famous for the extent of his improvisational boldness. He would embellish on the organ even in the middle of church services. In other performances, he would take musical themes tossed at him from the audience and immediately improvise around them, something more like a nightclub comic. Bach participated in improvisational duels with other musicians. And so it should be, as you play out each of your days.

Call and Response

Great time management is a conversation, not a monologue. Many people just walk through their day oblivious to those around them. The best time managers engage their day in dialogue. They ask for and wait for a response, holding the white spaces or silence until a partner steps up and grabs the microphone, owning his or her part.

The complexities of jazz, display call and response in many forms. It can be a dialogue between the pianists left hand and right hand, an exchange of the instrumentalist and vocalist or between a soloist and a choir. True jazz is always a conversation between the performers and the audience. A partnership is formed. The circle moves wider to include dancing of all kinds from free style to friendly games of leapfrog. It includes non-dancers too. Their focused attention and foot tapping become part of the performance. And so it is with time management. Is dancing, leapfrog or at least some toe tapping part of your day? Great time management is a made up conversation with your spouse, your customers and co-workers.

Daily Rhythm

Rhythm is everywhere in nature. The ebb and flow of the sea that Susy and I walk beside each day has a rhythm. There is the same rhythm each day, yet each day has subtle shifts.

There is a polyrhythmic quality to jazz that often follows an impulse to simultaneously play 4/4 alongside 3/4 and 6/8. Rhythm is also inextricably tied to pace. The rhythm seems to drive the music along in time, so much so, that it is often referred to as "keeping time". In one sense it creates time.

Every day has a pace and rhythm. Each has an optimal tempo that should be governed by the content, amount of information, and tools used. The pace should also be drawn from the emotional intent of each part of the day. Pay attention to the mood you want to create at any given point. This can include excitement, peace, laughter or suspense. But mostly, the pace and rhythm of a day needs to be informed by the intrinsic tempo of the individual activity. In the case of simultaneous multiple activities, there is a collective cadence that you want to discover and at least initially match.

I have made sales presentations with small children in the room. Not only were they not interested in my content, they were on a completely different pace than what was optimal for the presentation. I learned to keep a small set of crayons and some pages to color on with me in my briefcase at all times. I did everything I could to set them up with their own rhythm while I worked on a completely different one with their parents.

Selection and Creation of Venue

Every style of music has a venue type that is better suited for the style. Rock is big music that seems to work best in big venues like outdoor stadiums and huge indoor arenas. Classical works well in concert halls created for that type of music. To me, jazz works best in a more intimate "club" kind of environment. When I've experienced rock n roll in a small club, I seem to walk away with a headache. When a jazz ensemble advances in popularity to the point where they fill a huge venue, it seems like they lose something to the environment. It just doesn't work as well.

Beyond size, there are many other dimensions of environment that either enhance or detract from a performance. Everything possible should be considered to insure all the ingredients are working together to create an optimal outcome. Lighting, seating, color, texture, sound system, acoustics, and staging are only the beginning of considerations. What does the musician want the audience to feel or do? When they sell a song or a musical number, they are looking toward a particular response. The audience attends because they want to respond. What is that response? Toe tapping, clapping, dancing, singing along? Maybe the musician even wants the people to participate by purchasing a cd or t-shirt. In this case music becomes sales. Does the musician want everyone to return and pay to hear him play again? … More sales! Think through everything.

Your time management is no different. Venue selection and creation can make or break you. Pay attention to detail. Control what you can control. What size room is optimal? What are the acoustics? What are the seating arrangements? How many chairs are needed? Who should sit where? What about climate control? It's difficult to communicate, let alone sell, teach or inform, if people are too hot or too cold. Sometimes you have to play in the room you are given. But you can often get permission to create minor last minute adjustments that can make a huge difference.

Think of all the venues you play in during the day. Your office, your car, where you stop for lunch or breaks, where you meet your employees or prospective customers are all possibilities. Make sure your venues are well staged and orchestrated to set you up for success. Think about your instruments, song selection and set length.

Use Everything

There is a certain flexibility in jazz that allows the great musician to incorporate whatever happens to show up into a piece. Jazz great, and keyboard artist, Herbie Hancock played with the *Miles Davis Band.* Miles is on the short list of the greatest jazz musicians of all time. In his inspirational musical documentary, *Possibilities,* Herbie said, "Miles could use anything." He went on to explain, "Whatever another performer did, whatever showed up, Miles could masterfully work it into the piece and do it on the fly." Learn to use everything that shows up in a day. That's great time management.

CHAPTER 8

Your Daily *STRENGTHSPATH*

At the end of the day, the *STRENGTHSPATH* Principle is all about how you spend your days. No one has invented the shiny toy that makes up for the loss you feel when day after day you end up doing what you don't enjoy. Over the years I have collected dozens of examples of how successful people from a variety of professions spend their days. Here are four "day" samples. Some are very detailed. Each at least gives a feel for how that person regularly spends their time.

David Brenner, Comedian
"I have a routine I follow every day. About 3 o'clock I'll sit down with a stack of that day's newspapers and weekly magazines, and I'll go though it and clip stuff out that I think is interesting. And then I'll go on the internet and print out anything that might work from the fields of science or medicine or health. Initially, I might have no idea what I'm going to say about it; I just know that there's something there that could be funny. And then I'll watch *CNN* or another news channel and see what's happening there. And I make up these cards that have the story line on them. And then I go

on stage and hold up the card and hope something funny happens from it."

Michael Bloomberg, Financier, Mayor of New York

"I still think a perfect day is one where I'm hopelessly overscheduled. Jog early in the morning and get to work by 7:00 AM; a series of rushed meetings; phone call after phone call; fifty more voice messages and the same number of e-mails demanding a reply; a hurried business lunch between a myriad of stand-up conferences to solve personnel, financial, policy problems; perhaps give an interview to some foreign newspaper where we needed publicity; often make an image building speech at some local conference in person or by satellite video conferencing to the other side of the world; constantly welcome visiting clients; an early dinner with customers or a group of employees, followed by a second one with friends (where I actually get a chance to stop talking and eat); fall into bed, exhausted but satisfied with the day's accomplishments. That's the best weekday one could ever have!"

Maya Angelou, Poet, Novelist

"When I'm writing, everything shuts down. I get up about five, take a shower, and don't use the Rose Geranium bath gel from *Floris* – I don't want that sensual gratification. I get in my car and drive off to a hotel room. I can't write in my house. I take a hotel room and ask them to take everything off the walls so there's me, the Bible, Roget's Thesarus, and some good, dry sherry, and I'm at work by 6:30. I write on the bed lying down – one elbow is darker than the other, really black from leaning on it – and I write in longhand on yellow pads. Once I'm into it all disbelief is suspended, it's beautiful. I hate to go, but I've set for myself 12:30 as the time to leave, because after that it's an indulgence, it becomes stuff I'm going to edit out anyway.

Then back home, shower, fresh clothes, and I go shopping for nice food and pretend to be sane. After dinner I re-read what I've written... If April is the cruelest month, then eight o'clock at night is the cruelest hour, because that's when I start to edit and all that pretty stuff I've written gets axed out. So I've written 10 or 12 pages in six hours, it'll end up as three or four if I'm lucky.

But writing is really my life. Thinking about it when I'm not doing it is terribly painful, but when I'm doing it... it's a lot like if I was a long-distance swimmer and had to jump into a pool covered with ice: It sounds terrible, but once in it and two or three laps done, I'm home and free."

Warren Buffet, Investor

"Well, first of all, I tap-dance into work. And then I sit down and read. Then I talk on the phone for seven or eight hours. And then I take more home to read. Then I talk on the phone in the evening. We read a lot. We have a general sense of what we're after. We're looking for seven footers. That's about all there is to it... I am doing what I would like most to be doing in the world, and I have since I was 20. I choose to work with every single person I work with. That ends up being the most important factor. I don't interact with people I don't like or admire."

Design a *STRENGTHSPATH* Day

Wake Up

What time? 6am? 7am? 8am? When I feel like it?

What kind of alarm? Loud and annoying? Or calm and serene?

What's the first thing I do? Shower? Meditate? Exercise?

Pray? Read spiritual text? Have pillow talk?

What do I wear? Something different? Or the same thing?

Breakfast

Do I eat? Yes? No?

What do I eat? Cereal? Oatmeal? Yogurt? Smoothie?

Is it hot or cold?

Is it food or drink?

Is it healthy or just filling?

Coffee or no coffee?

Buy it or make it?

Eat with family or not?

Sit and eat or eat on the go?

Commute

Do I commute?

If so, how far? How long?

Car, carpool, walk, bike, train, or a combination?

Do I work from home?

What do I do during my commute? People watch? Read the news? Listen to audio books? Check email? Sleep?

Work

What time do I get in? 8am? 9am? 11am?

Do I plan my day or just let it come to me?

What's the first thing I do? Greet people? Check email? Design my day? Clear my desk?

When do I check email throughout the day? When it comes? When I have time? At certain times?

Do I take a break? If so, when? How often? How long?

What time do I leave work? 5pm? 6pm? When I'm done? When I'm tired? When my boss leaves?

Do I eat snacks? What kind? When?

Do I drink throughout the day? Water? Coffee? Soda? Juice?

Do I have uninterrupted work time? If so, when? Where? How long?

Do I prepare for tomorrow before I leave?

Lunch

Do I take lunch?

If so, what time?

How long?

Do I bring it or buy it?

Where? Outside? At my desk? In the cafeteria?

What do I do? Eat? Take a walk? Read? Call someone?

What do I eat?

Do I connect with someone?

Do I nap?

Do I run errands?

After Work

Do I go straight home?

Do I exercise? If so, how and how long? Bike? Run? Weight lift? Cross Fit? Yoga? Intramural sports?

Do I do something fun? A hobby? A movie? A bar? A date?

Do I continue my education? Reading? Online class?

Do I meet with someone? Friend? Mentor? Family?

Do I volunteer?

Do I call people I care about?

Do I go to the grocery store?

Do I buy take out?

Dinner

Do I eat dinner?

If so, what time?

What do I eat?

Do I cook it or buy it?

Do I eat with someone?

Do I eat and talk or do I eat and watch TV?

Do I cook something familiar or something new?

Before Bed

Do I do more work?

Do I check email?

Do I answer work calls?

Do I make personal calls?

Do I watch a favorite show or a new movie?

Do I take a bath or shower?

Do I pray?

Do I journal?

Do I write down what I'm grateful for?

What time do I go to sleep?

This will help you be more intentional about your day. When you intentionally design your day, you'll find yourself experiencing more perfect days.

"If today were the last day of your life, would you want to do what you are about to do today?"
~Steve Jobs

CHAPTER 9

Agile Time Management

Agile platforms are project management frameworks originated at *Toyota*, and are now being implemented by thousands of individuals, teams and organizations in all types of industries all over the world. In 1986, it took *General Motors* 40 hours to manufacture a car with an average of 13 defects per car. In the same year, *Toyota* could manufacture an equal car in 18 hours with 4.5 defects. What allowed *Toyota* to outperform *General Motors* at this level? There was only one significant difference. *Toyota* had been using an *Agile* project management framework known as *Lean*. In recent years, *General Motors* has used *Lean* to completely close that gap.

Building contractors now use *Agile* as do farmers, classroom teachers and wedding planners. *National Public Radio Teams* began using *Agile* strategies during the chaotic events of the Arab Spring. It has spread throughout the organization and then to teams at the *Washington Post*, *New York Times* and *Chicago Tribune*. The *Grameen Foundation* is using *Agile* methodologies to eliminate poverty in Uganda.

Agile Information Technology has diversified into multiple frameworks including *Extreme Programming*, *Kanban*, and *Scrum*. You can transform your time management using the same project management framework that the world's top companies are using to build products and services.

There are several benefits of the *Agile* framework. It's extremely flexible as the name implies and it's simple to start using. But when the need is there, it can expand into a very sophisticated set of tools. It can be used individually or with teams. If you are already using one of the *Agile* platforms in a work context, this will build on something you already understand. If you're not familiar with *Agile*, this provides a brief introduction that may benefit you later.

For a primer on *Agile Scrum*, I recommend Jeff Sutherland's book, *Scrum – The Art of Doing Twice the Work in Half the Time*. This is not your typical time management book. For a deeper dive, download the *SBOK Guide* or *Scrum Body of Knowledge*. It's free online. For an introduction to *Lean*, I recommend, *A Factory of One* by Daniel Markovitz.

On the following pages, I'm going to offer a very basic overview of *Agile*. I'm going to share 6 components. They are **Kanban Board**, **Sprint, Sprint Planning, Daily Scrum, Sprint Review and Sprint Retrospective**. If you want to start simply, for personal time management, just focus on the Kanban Board. This will offer a super simple fast start. (I am intentionally capitalizing all the *Agile* specific language that may be new to you.)

Kanban Board

"Write the vision and make it plain on tablets, that he may run who reads it."
~Habakkuk 2:2

Great time managers use scoreboards and dashboards to keep everyone aware of progress. Carl Pearson was the father of modern business statistics and is known for Pearson's Law: "When performance is measured, performance improves," and the corollary: "When performance is measured and reported, it improves exponentially." This is true even at the international economic level. The countries that measure and quantify have the strongest thriving economies.

In *Agile*, the project to-do list (called a Back-Log List) goes on a "Do" - "Doing" - "Done" board that is often referred to by the Japanese name Kanban (meaning "Card You Can See"). In the Scrum framework, it goes by Scrum Board.

I like the "Do" – "Doing" – "Done" format because it perfectly matches the **Y.E.S.** time frames I use in passion assessment. Is there a **Yearning** before you begin the items on the "Do" list? Is there **Engagement** with a growing sense of energy and timelessness while you're "Doing" the items? Is there a sense of **Satisfaction** after you've "Done" the items on the list? The Kanban Board can provide a terrific strengths check-in.

You can easily build your own Kanban on a sheet of paper, poster board, grease board or using an online tool. If you go with the online option, I recommend *Trello.com* which is what I use. It's easy to learn and can be reconfigured and shared easily.

Kanban Board		
Do	**Doing**	**Done**

Sprint

A Sprint is a time-boxed process of one month or less, where an individual or team implements a goal-oriented Backlog of Tasks. A common Sprint length is 21 days but it can be up to 30 days or as little as one week. If you're just introducing the concept, you can shorten your Sprint length to a single day or even an hour or less for a walk-through or training purposes. You can also combine it with the *Pomodoro* concept to work with 25 minute increments.

The idea of a Sprint is to completely finish an increment of a project. A personal Sprint could be completing a chapter of a book, losing 5 pounds or exercising 30 minutes a day for 21 days. The Sprint is all about having specific demonstrated results at the end. Some *Lean* practitioners use the term MVP for Minimum Viable Product to describe the end result. Minimum in this case does not refer to cutting corners or short cuts. It refers to delivering each project increment with a fully functional working product or service. By keeping the Sprint length short, course corrections and customer responsive adjustments can be made.

Sprint Planning

Each Sprint begins with a planning session. In the world of software design, a planning session for a 21 day Sprint might take 8 hours. You may spend much less time if you're using the *Agile* method for personal time management. I recommend the 1-week Sprint time frame for individual use in the beginning. When planning a Sprint segment, consider the **S.P.R.I.N.T.S.** acrostic below that is loosely built on the *Agile* pattern. Most of these ideas are pulled from the *Agile Scrum* family but some are pulled from *Lean*.

Story Map

Agile planning begins with a focus on how the product/ service will add value to a client, customer or specific end user. *Agile* planning starts with a 3-step **User Story** that is often placed on a simple 3x5 index card.

I am… Who is the client, customer or end user or what is their role? (Example: Secretary, Bookkeeper)

I want… What does the end user want the product/ service to achieve for them? (Example: Word Processing, Spread Sheet)

So that… What will be the benefit of that? (Example: Faster Document Preparation, Clear Accounting)

A Story Map includes a description of what will be delivered to the client or customer. *Agile* planning is very big on providing a very clear definition of "Done". The "Done" criteria should include quality standards. (Example: Software will include intuitive keyboard short cuts and be field tested and approved by secretaries.)

Deliverables are what will be delivered and demonstrated at the end of each Sprint. *Agile* often creates a Project Vision

Statement that explains the business need that will be met or what problem will be solved. (Example: We are creating a new software to enhance document preparation.)

The Shippable Product/Service or Deliverables are what will be demonstrated at the end of each Sprint. Story Maps are often used to give a visual outline of the product/service development sequence. This is similar to Storyboarding used by *Disney.* Value Stream Mapping may be used to identify non-value adding elements of a process.

Problems

A SWOT Analysis or a Force Field Analysis may be incorporated to identify potential obstacles and trouble. Threats are risks that could affect a project in a negative manner.

The Bruce Tuckman Norming - Forming - Storming - Performing group process model is often used to identify potential team conflicts.

In the *Lean* framework, Plan-Do-Check-Act may be implemented with problem solving. Other tools include the A-3 thinking and a tool called the 5 Whys. *Lean* adherents also follow the radical *Toyota* practice of allowing any worker on the assembly line to stop production and work on solving a problem.

Roles and Responsibilities

Agile planning then moves to identify the team members. In *Agile* Scrum the team has very specific names with very spelled out roles. I generally don't focus on the names like Scrum Master and Product Owner or Project Owner.

A Skills Requirement Matrix or framework can be used to identify skill gaps and training requirements for team members.

Agile is not inherently a strengths based project management system although many of the successful software companies like *Cisco* and *Facebook* are very strengths oriented. A basic tenet of Scrum is that all team members are cross-functional, that is, everyone has the skills necessary to complete any part of the Sprint. From a strengths perspective, this may not be optimal.

Agile projects can be completed without considering team member strengths and weaknesses. But virtually every top company, including *Toyota,* where the *Agile* concept was developed, is very strengths savvy. The tendency for mediocre companies is to focus solely on perceived skills as outlined on a resume and perceived knowledge as a function of a college degree. Great companies don't do that. Companies like *Toyota, Apple, Google* and *Facebook* look for Passion, Talent, Personality, Character and Values as well as Skill and Knowledge. I recommend constructing a Strengths Matrix to identify what/who you need on the team. *Facebook* is widely known to use a key strengths based question as a signature part of their interview process:

"On your very best day at work – the day you come home and think you have the very best job in the world – what did you do that day?"

The answer to that question will tell you so much whether you are hiring new employees or putting together the next project team.

Increments/Implementation/Iterations

Agile planning uses the term Iteration to describe the incremental segments within each Sprint. A Backlog or to-do list is built to describe the sequential tasks and activities that will go into the Sprint. These tasks go on a Burn Down Chart or Kanban Board. Again, with the online option, I recommend *Trello.com* which is what I use. It's easy to learn and can be reconfigured and shared easily.

Niche Work Space

I include an emphasis on the space where the work will be done. *Agile* Scrum often refers to the work space as the **War Room**. It is optimally designed in a way that all team members can move freely, communicate and get their work done. Recently, there has been some criticism leveled at software development companies suggesting that the often used "open work" spaces do not provide an optimized environment for what Cal Newport and others call "deep work". This should be a consideration and a quiet, less interactive work space may be included in some cases.

The *Lean* family uses the Japanese term **Gemba** when talking about the space where value is created. Gemba could be the factory floor, a construction site, a farm, the desk where you write, the classroom where you teach, or the territory where you sell. *Apple's* retail store could be thought of as their Gemba.

Time Estimate

Agile generally uses a team approach to estimating time and effort requirements on each Sprint. Estimating is not a top-down activity in *Agile*. The entire Sprint team is usually involved. Special *Agile* Poker Cards are often used as a method of identifying the amount of time that will be required for each task.

Sprint list items may be identified by difficulty. Fibonacci sequence numbers are often used for this: 0,1,1, 2, 3, 5, 8, 13, 21 and so on.

Wideband Delphi Technique is used to describe an anonymous estimation process. Team members anonymously provide estimates for each product/service feature. They then discuss factors influencing their time calculations and move on to a second round of anonymous estimates. The process is repeated until team members either develop consensus or get close to agreement.

Sprint Velocity is a term used to identify the rate at which the team can complete the work of a Sprint.

Productive Sustainable Pace suggests the rate a team can comfortably maintain.

S Framework

Agile Lean uses a methodology called 5S. They have corresponding Japanese terms but the English terms are *Sort, Set Up, Sweep, Standardize* and *Sustain*.

Sort means throwing out useless or obsolete items and organizing the remaining items by frequency of use.

Set Up is arranging the tools and materials to promote a smooth workflow. In construction, I referred to this as staging the job.

Sweep is the maintenance phase and includes keeping the workspace clean. I would refer to it as *Struggle* because it's my weakness.

Standardize means developing a systematic ongoing work process. Standardizing in the 5S sense is not static but open-ended including ongoing improvements.

Sustain means having an ongoing system for maintaining and upgrading the first four elements.

Daily Scrum (Standup Meeting)

Agile teams have daily 15 minute, standup meetings, often in front of the Kanban Board. *Trello* versions can be used for teams working remotely from different locations. The team reviews what was completed yesterday and previews what will be completed today. In some contexts, a set of 4 questions are used:

1. What has my team done since the last meeting?
2. What will my team do until the next meeting?
3. What are other teams counting on that remains undone?
4. What is the team doing that might affect other teams?

Some Scrum teams use a shorter 3 question model:

1. What did I complete yesterday?
2. What will I complete today?
3. What obstacles am I currently facing?

Sprint Review

The Sprint Review meeting is typically structured to last 1-4 hours and is scalable up or down depending on the length of the Sprint. The purpose is to demonstrate or present the deliverables, usually to the Product Owner.

Sprint Retrospective

The Sprint Retrospective is typically structured to last 1-4 hours and is also scalable up or down depending on the length of the Sprint. The purpose is to review the process of that particular Sprint, identify what was learned, and suggest improvements for future Sprints.

Some *Agile* Sprints include a Retrospective Kanban with four categories: "Went Well", "Needs to Change", "Question & Discussion", "Action Items".

Speed Boat is a technique often used to identify the improvements. Team members play the role of a crew on a Speed Boat. The boat's goal is to reach an island which symbolizes the Project's Vision Statement. Sticky notes or index cards are used to identify the project's engines (accelerators) and anchors (drag). Engines are the things that helped the Sprint team reach the island and anchors are the things that slowed them down. This exercise is usually Time-Boxed to a few minutes in length.

More Exponential Results

It is so easy to get lulled into believing that individuals can be replaced like parts in a machine. With people, there are wide variations in strengths and performance.

Jeff Sutherland, co-founder of the *Scrum Project Management System* offers the following true story in his book titled *Scrum – The Art of Doing Twice the Work in Half the Time.*

Professor Stanley Eisenstat has been the instructor in the notoriously difficult, *Computer Science 323* course at *Yale University.*

Former student turned tech entrepreneur, Joel Spolsky wanted to know if there was any correlation between time spent on class projects and the grade received. Spolsky discovered there was no correlation, but the results were more interesting than that.

He found the fastest "A" students outpaced the slower "A" students by an incredible 10:1 margin. In other words, they were 10x faster on class projects and got just as good of a grade.

Rapid learning and work pace are strong indicators of innate talent. In a rapidly changing world, you will want to focus on careers where you can learn new material in the shortest time and where you can complete tasks quickly and efficiently.

Research shows an even greater gap. Sutherland references a team study that surveyed 3,800 different projects in a wide variety of fields. At the team level, variance range for exactly the same work project was one week to two thousand weeks.

Like individuals and teams, project management systems are not all equally effective. In 2010, *Federal Bureau of Investigation* agents were still filing most of their reports on paper. This issue was a substantial factor in the circumstances leading up to the attack on the *World Trade Center* nine years earlier. The first attempt to fix this was scrapped after 3 years and 70 million dollars of taxpayer money. The second attempt was projected to cost over 400 million dollars. *Agile* project management was finally used by a third team that fully delivered the project in 20 months at a fraction of the budget.

The *Healthcare.gov* rollout began with a similar disaster. The team who fixed it used *Agile Scrum*. Great people using an inferior project management system will produce less than spectacular results.

Amazon founder Jeff Bezos was asked what he believed were the greatest changes he saw coming in the next few years. Bezos responded, "That's a good question but a great question is what won't change in the next few years?" Bezos continued, "What won't change is the desire to get products and services faster and at a lower cost."

Bezos is correct. Both of those desires are timeless. Your ability as an individual and team member to deliver a product or service faster and at a lower cost will always be in high demand. And they are a function of great time management.

AFTERWORD

Accumulation

Success strategist Brian Tracy talks about what he calls, "The Law of Accumulation". Tracy says, "Everything great and worthwhile in human life is an accumulation of hundreds and sometimes thousands of tiny efforts and sacrifices that nobody ever sees or appreciates...A snowball starts very small, but it grows as it adds millions and millions of tiny snowflakes, and continues to grow as it gathers momentum."

Your body of knowledge results from accumulating millions of small information pieces. Any person with a large knowledge base has spent thousands of hours building that knowledge one piece at a time. What you see when you meet that individual, is an expert in his or her field. It's that high level of knowledge that makes him extremely valuable in the marketplace.

Warren Buffett's daily routine includes a lot of reading. In fact, he spends about 80% of his day reading. And he does this *every* day. Buffett reportedly reads at least 3 annual reports (a couple of hundred pages each) every day. When asked how to get smarter he held up a stack of paper and said. "Read 500 pages like this every day. That's how knowledge builds up, like compound interest."

Accumulation applies in the area of experience. Successful people in any field are those who have far more experience in that field than the average. There is nothing that replaces experience. Nothing.

Good and bad time management accumulates. It compounds. You can waste time today and no one will probably notice. You can probably waste time all week and no one will notice. It's like gaining weight. You can overeat today and the most you would gain would be a pound or so. Your clothes will still fit. Even your spouse wouldn't know the difference. But after 3 months of overeating, you will have put on some serious weight.

What you are doing right now turns into minutes. Minutes turn into hours into days into months into years into a lifetime into a legacy... even an eternity. Investment of time pays off over time.

Tolstoy spent 6 years writing *War and Peace*. Da Vinci worked on the *Mona Lisa* four years as did Michelangelo painting the ceiling of the *Sistine Chapel*. Most people overestimate what they can accomplish in a single year and underestimate what they can accomplish in five years. It's accumulation.

Poorly used time accumulates as well. According to *Digital Trends*, Americans are spending an average of 4.7 hours a day on social media, much of it on their phones. Some of this is happening at work and is task avoidance. They are working at jobs that don't fit them. This time accumulates.

Many people start a time management program and they don't stick with it. I believe it's because <u>they believe</u> that good time management = discipline to do activities you hate. <u>From a strengths perspective, just the opposite is true</u>. <u>Good time management = doing what you love and are good at.</u> When that truth sinks into your bones and you begin to act on it, the law of accumulation will kick in as well.

Static and Dynamic Equilibrium

One problem with time is that it doesn't stay managed. In past workshops, I would bring in a bowl and a marble. Set a marble in a right side up bowl and it will stay there. Set a marble in an upside down bowl and it will keep rolling off. The right side up bowl represents "Static Equilibrium". You set something up and it stays set up. The upside down bowl represents "Dynamic Equilibrium". For the marble to stay on top the bowl, you must keep putting it up there.

Time management is a dynamic equilibrium activity. Time doesn't stay managed. It's like weight management. You don't expect your good eating habits from last month to help with your weight management this month. You have to get up and take action every day.

From a strengths perspective, managing time should be enjoyable. If you're going to stay with a positive eating plan, you'll need to find a number of foods that are healthy, low calorie and tasty! If you're going to stick with a positive time plan, productive activities need to be enjoyable and fit your natural talents. The time management strategies themselves must be enjoyable.

Whenever I coach a client, present a training program or sit down to write a book chapter, I am acutely aware that life is so much more complicated than the best advice I could offer. Any single piece of wisdom is always incomplete. Most groupings of wisdom are incomplete as well. This book is actually about 50% shorter than the one I originally wrote. I became convinced that many in my intended audience wouldn't read a longer book, at least initially. So you have the shortened version with some of the material left on the "cutting room floor".

I am also aware that most readers who start a book, don't finish it and fewer still actually implement even one of the ideas presented. Obviously that won't help.

The *STRENGTHSPATH TIME MANAGER* is an integrated, interdependent set of strategies. My observation and experience is that they work together synergistically. A lot has been written recently, pushing back on authors who encourage us to find and follow their passion. One book, *Do What You Love, The Money Will Follow* by Marsha Sinetar is an example. The title, while catchy, is incomplete. Sinetar's advice is way more detailed than the title suggests. I doubt the critics of her book have seriously put the suggestions to any serious test. Based on the shallow criticism I see, most haven't even read the first two chapters.

If you want to try these strategies using an a-la-carte process you can. But like the critics, I think you'll be disappointed. Passion without talent, skill and knowledge doesn't get you very far. If you have those four components, but try to implement them in an organizational culture where you are misaligned, you will still beat your head against the wall. That's why I didn't write a book encouraging you to simply find and follow your passion. It's not because it doesn't work, it's just incomplete!

I will close the book with one last thought. At the end of the day, time management is about making choices. Should I do this or that? Should I increase the time spent on one activity and decrease the time spent on another? In my own life, I find that God is willing to offer help with these decisions including the little ones. As an imperfect follower of Jesus, I try to live my days in constant communication with God through the One referred to in Scripture as Holy Spirit. I frequently ask Him, "Should I do this or that?" Although I don't claim to hear an audible voice, somewhere deep in my spirit, I believe I get direction on matters both large and small.

I also try to spend part of everyday reading and thinking about a section of Scripture. Susy and I usually start our day together in this way. I believe it grounds us, gets us on the same page with each other, and with God. The Bible is full of great time-life management tips. That's where I got my introduction to strengths. And it not only emphasizes the importance of priorities, but offers clear direction on what the priorities should be for a well-lived life.

When I was very young, my mother helped me memorize a short passage of Scripture from the book of Proverbs. Susy and I have that passage framed in our entry way. It reads, "Trust in the Lord with all your heart and don't lean on your own understanding. In all your ways acknowledge God and He will direct your paths."

~See You On The Path!!!

Dale Cobb

BIBLIOGRAPHY

Prologue

Introduction

1. Zig Ziglar, *See You At The Top* (Gretna, Louisiana: Pelican Publishing, 1977), 6.

2. Kip Tindell, *Uncontainable: How Passion, Commitment, and Conscious Capitalism Built a Business Where Everyone Thrives* (New York: Hachette Book Group, 2014), 53.

Chapter 1   Your Signature Strengths

1. Oprah Winfrey, *The Best of Oprah's What I Know For Sure* (New York: The Oprah Magazine, Hearst Corporation, 2000), 39.

2. Bob McDonald and Don E. Hutcheson, *Don't Waste Your Talent* (Marietta, Georgia: Longstreet Press, 2000), xi.

3. Howard Gardner, *Multiple Intelligences* (New York: Basic Books, New York, 1993), 17-26.

4. Margaret E. Broadley, *Your Natural Gifts* (McLean, Virginia: EPM Publications, 1977), 3-7.

5. Richard "Mack" Machowicz, *Unleash The Warrior Within* (New York: Philadelphia, Da Capo Press/Perseus Books, 2008), 141.

6. Ben Carson with Gregg Lewis & Deborah Shaw Lewis, *You Have A Brain* (Grand Rapids: Zondervan, 2015), 90-93.

7. Peter Drucker, *Managing Oneself* (Boston: Harvard Business Review, 2008),11-19.

8. Marcus Buckingham, *StandOut 2.0* (Boston: One Thing Productions/Harvard Business School Publishing, 2015), 8.

9. Stephen M.R. Covey with Rebecca Merrill, *The Speed of Trust* (New York: Free Press/Simon and Schuster, 2001).

10. Tom Rath and Barry Conchie, *Strengths Based Leadership* (New York: Gallup Press, 2008), 24.

11. Jim Loehr, *The Only Way To Win: How Building Character Drives Higher Achievement and Greater Fulfillment in Business and Life* (New York: Hyperion, 2012).

Chapter 2   Your Signature Targets

1. Kip Tindell, *Uncontainable: How Passion, Commitment, and Conscious Capitalism Built a Business Where Everyone Thrives* (New York: Hachette Book Group, 2014), 53.

2. *Going to A Higher Authority* (USA Today, May 28, 1999).

3. Tony Robbins, *Unlimited Power: The Way to Peak Personal Achievement* (New York: Fawcett Columbine, 1986), 199.

4. Earl Nightingale, *Lead the Field* Audio Program (Chicago: Nightingale-Conant, 1977).

5. Gerald Sindell, *Discover Your Genius* (New York: MJF Books, Fine Communications, 2009), 23-25.

6. Earl Nightingale, *The River or the Goal* (Chicago: Nightingale-Conant), http://www.nightingale.com/articles/the-river-or-the-goal/.

7. Interview with Diane Sawyer (US Magazine, 1997).

8. Interview with Ellen Barkin (Parade Magazine, June 8, 2016).

9. Pablo Picasso Quote from Rodney King, *Is Thinking Like an Artist The Key To Success for Entrepreneurs?* (Successfastlane.com, December 27, 2015), http://successfastlane.com/2015/12/27/is-thinking-like-an-artist-the-key-to-success-for-entrepreneurs/.

10. Isabel Allende Quote from Robert S. Root-Bernstein, Michele M. Root-Bernstein, *Sparks of Genius: The Thirteen Thinking Tools of the World's Most Creative* (New York: Houghton Mifflin, 2001), 9.

11. Girl Scout, CEO Frances Hesselbein Story from Rick Smith, *The Leap* (New York: Penguin Group, 2009), 52-55.

12. Interview with Lori Greiner (Dallas: Success Magazine, February 2016).

13. Richard Eyre, *Spiritual Serendipity, Cultivating and Celebrating the Art of the Unexpected* (New York: Simon and Schuster, 1997).

14. Morton A. Myers M.D., *Happy Accidents – Serendipity in Major Medical Breakthroughs in the Twentieth Century* (New York: Arcade Publishing, 2011).

15. Bobb Biehl, *Stop Setting Goals – If You Would Rather Solve Problems* (Nashville: Moorings Publishing, 1995).

16. Stephen Covey, *Seven Habits of Highly Effective People* (New York: Free Press, A division of Simon & Schuster, 2004).

17. Victor Frankl, *Man's Search for Meaning* (Boston: Beacon Press, 2014).

18. Interview with Tim Ferris (Dallas: Success Magazine, November 2015).

19. Song Title – *It's The Climb,* performed by Miley Cyrus, written by Jessi Alexander and Jon Mabe (Walt Disney Records, March 12, 2009).

20. Jim Hayhurst, Sr., *The Right Mountain – Lessons from Everest On the Real Meaning of Success* (Etobicoke, Ontario: John Wiley & Sons, 1997).

21. Parker J. Palmer, *Let Your Life Speak: Listening for the Voice of Vocation* (San Francisco: Jossey-Bass, John Wiley & Sons, 2000), 3.

22. Tim Ferris, *The 4-Hour Work Week* (New York: Crown Publishers, 2009).

Chapter 3 Your Signature Routes

1. John Maxwell, *Today Matters - 12 Daily Practices to Guarantee Tomorrow's Success* (New York: Time Warner Book Group, 2004), 69.

2. Interview with Tony Robbins (Dallas: Success Magazine, January 2015).

3. Marcus Buckingham & Curt Coffman, *First, Break All The Rules* (New York: Simon & Schuster, 1999), 117.

4. Lee Iacocca, William Novak, *Iacocca: An Autobiography* (New York, Bantam Books, 2004), 21.

5. Scott Adams Quote from Daniel H. Pink, *Drive: The Surprising Truth About What Motivates Us* (New York: Riverhead Books/Penguin 2009), 99.

6. Mason Currey, *Daily Rituals – How Artists Work* (New York: Alfred Knopf, 2014).

7. Movie Quote, *City Slickers* (Beverly Hills: Castlerock Entertainment, 1991).

8. Covert Bailey, *Fit or Fat Target Diet* (Boston: Houghton Mifflin, 1984).

9. Alex Guerrero, *In Balance for Life: Understanding and Maximizing Your Body's pH Factor* (New York: Square One Publishers, 2005).

10. Arianna Huffington Interview with Darren Hardy, http://darrenhardy.com/2014/08/wow-productivity/.

11. Vishen Lakhiani, *The Code of the Extraordinary Mind* (New York: Rodale, 2016).

12. Matthew E. May, *The Elegant Solution: Toyota's Formula for Mastering Innovation* (New York: Free Press/Simon & Schuster, 2007), xi.

Chapter 4   Classic Time Management - Revised

1. Bill Clinton, *My Life: The Early Years* (New York: Vintage Books/Random House), 3.

2. Alan Lakein, *How To Get Control Of Your Time And Your Life* (New York: Peter H. Wyden, 1973), 99.

3. Peter Bregman, *18 Minutes – Find Your Focus, Master Distraction and Get the Right Things Done* (New York: Hachette Books, 2011), 136.

4. Richard Branson, *How I've Survived, Had Fun, and Made a Fortune Doing Business My Way* (New York: Crown Publishing, 2007).

5. Bill Gates, *How I Work* (New York: Fortune Magazine republished by CNN Money, April 7, 2006), http://money.cnn.com/2006/03/30/news/newsmakers/gates_howiwork_fortune/.

6. Earl Nightingale, *The 25 Thousand Dollar Idea* (Chicago: Nightingale-Conant), www.**nightingale**.com/articles/the-**25000**-**idea**.

7. Richard Lieder, *Life Skills: Taking Charge of Your Personal and Professional Growth* (New York: Pfeiffer, 1996).

8. David Allen, *Getting Things Done: The Art of Stress Free Productivity* (New York: Viking, 2001), 50-51.

9. Jim Koch, *The 80/20 Principle: The Secret of Achieving More With Less* (New York: Currency/Double-Day, 1998).

10. Jack Welch with Suzy Welch, *Winning* (New York: Harper Collins, 2005).

11. Tony Robbins, *Unlimited Power: The Way to Peak Personal Achievement* (New York: Fawcett Columbine, 1986).

12. Interview with Sara Blakely (Dallas: Success Magazine, January 2016).

13. B.C. Forbes, *In Budgeting Your Days, Allow Time For Thinking,* from *The Book of Business Wisdom,* Peter Krass, Editor (New York: John Wiley & Sons, 1997), 311-313.

14. IBM Archives, *A Culture of Think,* http://www-03.ibm.com/ibm/history/ibm100/us/en/icons/think_culture/transform/.

15. John Maxwell, *Today Matters - 12 Daily Practices to Guarantee Tomorrow's Success* (New York: Time Warner Book Group, 2004), 149.

16. Francesco Cirillo, *The Pomodoro Technique,* http://pomodorotechnique.com/get-started/.

17. R. Alec Mackenzie, *Time Traps* (New York: Amacom, 1990), 55.

18. Eric Abrahamson and David H. Freedman, *A Perfect Mess* (New York: Back Bay/Little Brown & Company, 2007).

19. Vishen Lakhiani, *The Code of the Extraordinary Mind* (New York: Rodale, 2016), 129.

20. Jessica Hische, *In Progress: See Inside a Lettering Artist's Sketchbook and Process, from Pencil to Vector* (San Francisco: Chronicle Books, 2015).

21. Christine Mims, *"Passion Clumps" Concept,* http://therevolutionaryclub.com.

22. Merlin Mann, *(10+2)*5 Concept, 43folders.com,* http://www.43folders.com/2005/10/11/procrastination-hack-1025

23. Brian Tracy, *Eat That Frog: 21 Ways to Stop Procrastinating and Get More Done In Less Time* (New York: Berrett Koehler, 2007).

24. Albert Gray, *The Common Denominator of Success, http://www.amnesta.net/mba/thecommondenominatorofsuccess-albertengray.pdf.*

25. Mark Zuckerberg, *Inc Magazine,* Article by Kevin Daum, *26 Inspiring Quotes From Facebook Founder Mark Zuckerberg,* http://www.inc.com/kevin-daum/26-inspiring-quotes-from-facebook-mogul-mark-zuckerberg.html.

26. John Maxwell, *The 21 Irrefutable Laws of Leadership* (Nashville: Thomas Nelson, 2007), 165.

27. Dave Grant, *The Ultimate Power* (Old Tappan: Fleming H. Revell, 1983), 145.

28. Dan Sullivan, *The Multiplier Mindset, We're on a WinStreak™! Are you?* By Strategic Coach, http://blog.strategiccoach.com/winstreak/.

Chapter 5   How I Manage Time

1. Rich Fettke, *Extreme Success: The 7-Part Program That Shows You How to Succeed Without Struggle* (New York: Fireside/Simon & Schuster, 2002).

2. Richard A. Swenson, *Margin: Restoring Emotional, Physical, Financial, And Time Reserves To Overloaded Lives* (Colorado Springs, NavPress, 1992).

3. Jim Fannin, *S.C.O.R.E. For Life: The Secret Formula for Thinking Like a Champion* (New York: Harper-Collins, 2005).

4. Tony Schwartz and Jim Loehr, *The Power of Full Engagement: Managing Energy, Not Time, Is the Key*

to High Performance and Personal Renewal (New York: Free Press/Simon & Schuster, 2003).

5.   Bobb Biehl, *Team Profile 2,* The Consulting Institute, http://bobbbiehl.com/product/team-profile-2/.

6.   *Seth Godin Blog*, August 6, 2016, http://sethgodin. typepad.com/seths_blog/2016/08/scientist-engineer-and-operations-manager.html.

7.   Ted Williams with John Underwood and Robert Cupp, *The Science of Hitting* (New York: Touchstone/Simon & Schuster, 2013).

8.   Rheta Grimsley Johnson, *Good Grief: The Story of Charles M. Schulz* (Kansas City: Andrews and McMeel, 1995).

9.   Ralph Roberts, *Walk Like A Giant, Sell Like A Madman: America's #1 Salesman Shows You How To Sell Anything!* (Hoboken: John Wiley & Sons, 2008).

10. Pete Carroll with Yogi Roth, *Win Forever: Live, Work and Play Like a Champion* (New York: Penguin Books, 2011), 114.

11. Rosamond Stone Zander, *Pathways to Possibility: Transforming Our Relationships with Ourselves, Each Other, And The World* (New York: Viking, 2016), 106.

12. Song Title – *You Can Take The Weather With You,* performed by Jimmy Buffett, originally performed by Crowded House, written by Neil Finn and Tim Finn (RCA Records, 2006).

13. Photo of John F. Kennedy and John Jr. in the Oval Office, https://iconicphotos.wordpress.com/2010/09/03/john-f-kennedy-jnr-under-the-resolute-desk/.

14. Mark Di Vincenzo, *Buy Ketchup In May And Fly At Noon* (New York: Harper Collins, 2009).

15. *"The sons of Issachar understood the times and knew what Israel should do..."* This passage from I Chronicles 12:32 is taken from the New King James Version published by Thomas Nelson.

16. Stephan Rechtschaffen, *Time Shifting: Creating More Time To Enjoy Your Life* (New York: Double Day, 1996).

Chapter 6   Shifting to Strengths

1. Joan Biskupic, *Personalities Shape Questioning* (USA Today, October 19, 2009), *http://www.usatoday.com/printedition/news/20091019/courtargues19_st.art.htm*.

2. Michael Burleigh, *An American Triple Threat: Eisenhower, Patton, and Bradley* (Wall Street Journal, April, 2011), http://online.wsj.com/article/SB1000142405 27487038063045762366333362199332.html.

3. Robert Schuller, *If It's Going To Be It's Up To Me* (San Francisco: Harper), 138.

4. Johnny Carson Quote, http://www.quotationspage.com/quote/2965.html.

5. Patrick McGinnis, *The 10% Entrepreneur* (New York: Portfolio/Penguin/Random House, 2016).

6. Rick Smith, *The Leap* (New York: Portfolio/Penguin/Random House, 2009).

7. Jack Welch with Suzy Welch, *Winning* (New York: Harper Collins, 2005).

Chapter 7   Time Management Jazz

1. Eric Abrahamson and David H. Freedman, *A Perfect Mess* (New York: Back Bay/Little Brown & Company, 2007).

2. Herbie Hancock: *Possibilities DVD* (New York: Vector Recordings, April 18, 2006).

Chapter 8   Your Daily STRENGTHSPATH

1. David Brenner, *David Brenner's Day*, Comedian (America West Magazine, April 2001).

2. Michael Bloomberg, *Bloomberg by Bloomberg* (New York: John Wiley & Sons, 2001).

3. Maya Angelou, *Maya Angelou's Day* (Utne Reader, July-August 1998).

4. Siimon Reynolds, Compiler, *Thoughts of Chairman Buffett* (New York: Harper Collins, 1998).

Chapter 9   Agile Time Management

1. Hirotaka Takeuchi and Ikujiro Nonaka, *The New New Product Development Game* (Boston: Harvard Business Review, January 1986), https://hbr.org/1986/01/the-new-new-product-development-game

2. Tycho Press, *Scrum Basics: A Very Quick Guide to Agile Project Management* (Berkeley: Tycho Press, 2015).

3. Jeff Sutherland, *Scrum: The Art of Doing Twice the Work in Half the Time* (New York: Crown Business, 2014).

4. Tridibesh Satpathy - Lead Author, *Scrum Study: A Guide to the Scrum Body of Knowledge* (Phoenix: Scrumstudy, 2013).

5. *"Write the vision and make it plain on tablets, that he may run who reads it."* This passage from Habakkuk 2:2 is taken from the New King James Version published by Thomas Nelson.

6. Jim Benson, Tonianne DeMaria Barry, *Personal Kanban: Mapping Work | Navigating Life* (Seattle: Modus Operandi Press, 2009).

7. Daniel Markovitz, *A Factory of One: Applying Lean Principles to Banish Waste and Improve Personal Performance* (Boca Raton: CRC Press, 2012).

Afterword

1. Brian Tracy, *The Great Little Book On Universal Laws of Success* (Franklin Lakes, Career Press, 1997), 74.

2. Lula Chang, *Americans Spend an Alarming Amount of Time Checking Social Media on their Phones* (Digital Trends, June 13, 2015), http://www.digitaltrends.com/mobile/informate-report-social-media-smartphone-use/.

3. J. Howard Grant, *Balancing Life's Demands: A New Perspective on Priorities* (Colorado Springs: Multnomah Press, 1986).

4. Marsha Sinetar, *Do What You Love, The Money Will Follow: Discovering Your Right Livelihood* (New York: Dell Books, 1989).

Also by Dale Cobb

*The STRENGTHSPATH Principle: Your
Roadmap to Career Success*

Look for these coming titles in the

SUCCESSPATH Series:

The STRENGTHSPATH Guide to Selection and Hiring

*The SUCCESSPATH Strategies: A Guide
To Universal Success Principles*

*The STRENGTHSPATH Strategies:
Succeeding by Doing What You Do Best*

*Crazy Good: A STRENGTHSPATH Guide
to Discovering Your Natural Talents*

*Insanely Great: A STRENGTHSPATH Guide
to Developing Your Talents Into Strengths*

*Wildly Successful: A STRENGTHSPATH Guide
to Delivering Your Strengths in the Workplace*

The STRENGTHSPATH Manager & Leader

The STRENGTHSPATH Sales Person

The STRENGTHSPATH Parent

*Maximize Your Ministry: A STRENGTHSPATH
Guide to Doing What You Do Best*

The STRENGTHSPATH Educator

The Daily STRENGTHSPATH

SUCCESSPATH Sprint Coaching

One-to-One Sprints ✫ 60-Minute Seminars ✫ Workshops

Modeling Projects ✫ Performance Research

Strengths Assessments ✫ Selection ✫ Outplacement

Strengths Oriented Career Development Sprints
Arrive! - Strengths Oriented Goal Sprints
Strengths Oriented Time Management Sprints
"A-Game" Sprints
Service Oriented Selling Sprints
Storyboarding – Customer Experience Journey Sprints

Connect Online

Follow Our SUCCESSPATH Sixty Second Seminars
LinkedIn https://www.linkedin.com/in/dalecobb
Facebook https://www.facebook.com/
successpathcareerdevelopment/
Twitter https://twitter.com/strengthspath
Website http://www.successpathcareerdevelopment.com
Vimeo https://vimeo.com/dalecobb
YouTube https://www.youtube.com/user/daleacobb
Tumblr https://www.tumblr.com/blog/dalecobb

Contact

Dale Cobb
P.O. Box 870
Grover Beach, CA 93483
805.668.9600

STRENGTHS DEFINITIONS

Contribution (Result, Benefit, Added Value, Difference Maker, Helpfulness, Significance, Deliverables, Profit, Performance, Solutions) Contribution is what you provide that helps attain an end result. It's the positive change that happens when you walk in the room, when you join a business unit, team or organization.

Passion (Intense Interests, Enthusiasm, Desire, Ambition, Love, Fascinations, Magnificent Obsession, Energy, Excitement) Passions are activities and subjects that make you feel strong. They may include willingness to sacrifice and suffer.

Talent (Natural Ability, Aptitude, Gift, Knack, Flair, Bent, Instinct, Genius, Inclination, Brilliance, Forte, Aptness) Talent is innate ability making performance and excellence at specific tasks easier. It also makes skill and knowledge acquisition easier with a specific domain.

Personality (Temperament, Preferences, Style, Nature, Disposition, Traits, Persona, Psyche) Personality is the organization of an individual's distinct traits and temperament.

Values (Priorities, Motivation, Beliefs, Ideals, What's Important) Values combine to build culture within an organization.

Learning Style (Perception, Organization, Retention and Response to Instruction Methods) Your learning path is your optimized pattern of acquiring and processing information.

Skills (Developed Ability, Mastery, Proficiency, Competency, Know-How, How-To including Methods, Steps, Sequences, Tool Use, Technology Use) Skills are abilities developed through deliberate systematic effort, intentional practice and often supported by training and coaching.

Knowledge (General Vocabulary, Professional Language, Industry Terminology, Rules, Regulations, Laws, Principles, Theories) Knowledge is acquired information, facts, understanding and comprehension of a subject.

Character (Honor, Morals, Ethics, Standards, Right/Wrong, Dependability, Attendance, Promptness) Character is keeping commitments, agreements and striving for excellence.

Collection - Other Strengths (Geography, Chronotype, Climate, Seasons, Pace, Spiritual Gifts, Experience, School, Bandwidth, Thinking Style, Tools, Tribe, Adversities, Disabilities) A strength is any resource, internal or external that can be turned into a marketplace contribution.

STRENGTHS SUMMARY

Contribution

Passion	Talents	Personality

Values	Learning Style	Skills

Knowledge	Character	Collection